W9-CXM-049

BACKGROUNDS TO DISPENSATIONALISM

BACKGROUNDS TO DISPENSATIONALISM

*ITS HISTORICAL GENESIS AND
ECCLESIASTICAL IMPLICATIONS*

by

CLARENCE B. BASS

ASSOCIATE PROFESSOR OF SYSTEMATIC THEOLOGY
BETHEL THEOLOGICAL SEMINARY
ST. PAUL, MINNESOTA

*Wm. B. Eerdmans Publishing Company
Grand Rapids, Michigan*

236.33
B 293

148118

© Wm. B. Eerdmans Publishing Co. 1960
All rights reserved

First edition, May 1960
Printed in the United States of America
Library of Congress Catalog Card Number 60-12924

To my wife

DORIS

*whose unselfish devotion and abiding loyalty
has enhanced ten years of marriage
into a millennium of joy*

INTRODUCTION

As with every system of theology, dispensationalism cannot be adequately evaluated apart from the personages involved in it, the times and events out of which it grew, and its presuppositions. Furthermore, it cannot be divorced either from the implications it has for the whole of theological thought and the practical consequences it has for contemporary church life, or from the conclusions that it logically draws concerning other systems of interpretation.

The purpose of this book is to explain the historical setting out of which dispensationalism has grown, and to analyze its implications. The book begins with the premise, which is later developed, that dispensationalism, as a system of theological interpretation, dates from the nineteenth century and that it was not known before in the history of Christian thought. It argues that *as a system of thought* dispensationalism can be traced to the theology and practice of John Nelson Darby, which was formulated in an atmosphere of theological controversy. It shows that this background is significant in understanding dispensationalism, and that only against this background can its implications and conclusions be seen in their proper perspective.

The plan of the book follows a single and direct approach. After defining dispensationalism by distinguishing it from the historic view of the church, it attempts, in summary form, to show the ways in which dispensationalism departs from the views that have characterized the historic premillennial faith.

Turning to the historical setting out of which dispensationalism arose, this study traces the development of the theology and practice of John Darby through the rise of the Plymouth Brethren movement, of which Darby has been universally acknowledged as the synthesizer. Every facet of the development of Darby's personality traits and of the Plymouth Brethren controversies is explored, since the author feels that these factors are fundamental in understanding the development of the principles of interpretation of dispensationalism.

Darby's doctrine of the church is analyzed to determine both

the presuppositions that influenced his concept of the difference between the church and Israel, and the implications that
this concept had upon the conduct of the church. This concept, conjoined with the actions of those involved in the
controversies, is viewed as establishing the principles to which
the separatist movement in some contemporary church groups
can be traced.

Against this concept of the church, the inherent eschatological views of Darby and dispensationalism are delineated. Their
contrast with the historic view and their implications for the
present form the basis upon which some arresting and thought-
provoking questions are drawn.

The book is not written in an argumentative manner. At
all times an effort has been made to deal fairly and objectively
with the ideas and events that come into view. The purpose
is not to construct a case against dispensationalism, but dis-
passionately and objectively to seek to determine the historical
genesis of this system of thought, which has had such an effect
upon the church, and to analyze its implications for contemporary church life. It is hoped that an unbiased approach to
the conclusion reached in this book will cause many seriously
to evaluate their relation to dispensationalism.

The book has in view only one kind of dispensationalist,
though there are really three types: the ultra-dispensationalist,
who becomes involved in fanciful excursions into the extremes;
the academic dispensationalist, who develops a full system of
dispensational truth, with all details carefully worked out;
and the pastor-dispensationalist. The pastor-dispensationalist
is one who has been taught the dispensational system in seminary, or Bible school, or has learned it from the Scofield Bible.
He believes tenaciously in the pretribulation rapture as the
blessed hope of the church. He may use the dispensational
charts when he speaks on Christ's second coming, but he has
not fully worked through to either the underlying presuppositions or the implications of dispensationalism. He will readily
protest that he does not believe some of the distinguishing
features of dispensationalism.

It is this pastor-dispensationalist for whom the book has been
written. The presuppositions and implications of dispensationalism are delineated so that he may evaluate how closely
this system adheres to a truly biblical interpretation and to

the historic faith of the church. The book is not, therefore, to be taken as a refutation of the academic dispensationalist. It is designed only to help the pastor-dispensationalist to understand the system.

Perhaps an autobiographical word may help the reader. I was reared in the dispensational system, and the formative years of my spiritual development occurred under the ministry of a godly pastor who taught it, complete with charts. I progressed through my entire college and seminary career without ever knowing that there was a distinction between dispensationalism and premillennialism. When I began a doctoral program of research on J. N. Darby's doctrine of the church I was a confirmed dispensationalist. As I began to understand the basis in which this system of interpretation is rooted, I began also to see what seemed to be a basic hermeneutical pattern of interpretation that is broadly divergent from that of the historic faith.

I have not found the way out of dispensationalism easy, and I sometimes wonder if even now I have left it completely. The inward struggle to orient oneself to the historic faith only, intensely involves many emotions. Moreover, readjusting theological patterns sometimes leaves one uncomfortable. Even today some of my dearest friends are convinced that I have departed from the evangelical faith. No affirmation of my belief in the cardinal doctrines of the faith — the virgin birth, the efficaciousness of Christ's death, the historicity of the resurrection, the necessity of the new birth, even the fervent expectancy of the personal, literal, actual, bodily return of the Lord to the earth — will convince them, because I have ceased to "rightly *divide* the word of truth."

I bear testimony, however, that the unity of the divine redemptive plan is now meaningful to me. The church, as the body of Christ providentially redeemed, is the epitome of the whole structure of God's purposes on the earth. This is truly the blessed hope.

The account of the historical events presented in this book has not been hastily constructed. It is the result of an intensive and exhaustive search for accuracy of detail that has taken the author into primary and secondary sources from the musty archives of research libraries to the private collections of those related to the events described herein. The record has been accredited to be "the most unbiased and accurate account yet written." I mention this only to emphasize the importance of understanding the historical background out of which dispensationalism has grown.

I wish to express my appreciation to Professor F. F. Bruce, Rylands Professor of Biblical Literature and Exegesis, University of Manchester, and to Geoffrey Williams, Esq., of the Evangelical Library London, for very valuable aid in obtaining primary materials; to the officials and staff of the National Library of Scotland, Edinburgh; New College Library, Edinburgh; the Scottish Central Library, Dunfermline; the Edinburgh Public Library, Edinburgh; the British Museum Library, London; the Bodleian Library, Oxford; and the Middlesborough Public Library, Middlesborough, for their assistance in the location and use of materials contained in this study; and to the Rev. Principal Charles Duthie, D.D., of the Scottish Congregational Seminary and the Post-Graduate School of Theology, New College, University of Edinburgh, under whose guidance this study was initiated.

NOTE: *The Collected Writings of J. N. Darby,* edited by William Kelly (London: G. Morrish, 1867-83, 32 vols.), are divided into eight categories. In making reference to these, the following abbreviations have been used: Col. Writ. for *Collected Writings;* Eccl. for Ecclesiastical; Doc. for Doctrinal; Exp. for Expository; Pro. for Prophetic; Prac. for Practical; Cri. for Critical; Evan. for Evangelistic; and Apol. for Apologetic. In each reference, the volume number indicates the volume within the category cited, and the page number indicates the page of the volume cited.

CONTENTS

CHAPTER I

THE DISTINGUISHING FEATURES OF DISPENSATIONALISM

No SURVEY of the history of the development of prophetic thought can long ignore the fact that certain features of a widely held system of prophetic interpretation vary markedly from the interpretation that has historically been held by the church. This system has evolved from its early digression from historic eschatological theology to a full-orbed theology that has all but replaced the historic views in certain circles. This system of interpretation is known as dispensationalism.

Dispensationalists have attempted repeatedly to demonstrate that both the chronology and method of dispensationalism may be traced back to the theology of the apostolic church. An example of this is found in *The Basis of the Premillennial Faith* by C. H. Ryrie. The author asserts that "premillennialism is the historic faith of the church,"[1] and he then proceeds to identify this historic belief in a premillennial return of the Lord with dispensationalism by asserting that "opponents of the premillennial system have attempted to obscure the main issues involved by inventing distinctives between historic premillennialists, pretribulationists, dispensationalists, and ultra-dispensationalists. Such distinctions are not warranted since the differences are minor. . . ."[2] Assuming that premillennialism and dispensationalism are synonymous terms, he traces numerous references in the history of the church to such terms as "second advent," "chiliasm," "millennial," "thousand years," "tribulation," "kingdom on earth," "Antichrist," etc. to establish the continuity between dispensationalism and the historic views of the church.

Other dispensational writers follow the same approach. Sil-

1. C. H. Ryrie, *The Basis of the Premillennial Faith.* New York: Loizeaux Brothers, 1953, p. 17.
2. *Ibid.,* p. 12.

vers contends that the Apostolic Fathers "expected the return of the Lord in their day . . . they taught the doctrine of the imminent and premillennial return of the Lord."[3]   Stanton appeals to Harnack, "a member of the liberal theological school, [who] out of sheer honesty as a historian . . . writes, 'In the history of Christianity . . . [there is] a belief in the speedy return of Christ and in His glorious reign on earth.' "[4]

Many similar attempts to identify dispensationalism with the historic belief in the personal, literal return of Christ to reign on the earth could be cited. This type of approach, however, only begs the question. There is unanimous agreement that the apostles and early Church Fathers readily believed and proclaimed the return of the Lord to the earth and His future personal reign on the earth.   No dispensational writer has ever been able to offer, however, a single point of continuity between what is today known as dispensationalism and the historic premillennial view.

George Ladd, an avowed premillennialist, after an intensive survey of the eschatological writings in the history of the church, with particular reference to the Church Fathers, concludes:

> In this survey of the early centuries we have found that the church interpreted the book of Revelation along futuristic lines: i.e., they understood the book to predict the eschatological events which would attend the end of the world. . . . God would purify the Church through suffering, and Christ would save her by His return at the *end of the tribulation* when He would destroy Antichrist, deliver His Church, and bring the world to an end and inaugurate His millennial kingdom. The prevailing view is a post-tribulation premillennialism. *We can find no trace of pretribulationism in the early church*: and no modern pretribulationist has successfully proved that this particular doctrine was held by any of the church fathers or students of the Word *before the nineteenth century*.[5]

This same conclusion is reached by John Wick Bowman, noted New Testament scholar, who writes:

3. Jesse Forest Silvers, *The Lord's Return: Seen in History and in Scripture as Premillennial and Imminent*. New York: Fleming H. Revell Co., 1914, pp. 62, 64.

4. Gerald B. Stanton, *Kept From the Hour*. Grand Rapids: Zondervan Publishing House, 1956, p. 126.

5. George Eldon Ladd, *The Blessed Hope*. Grand Rapids: Wm. B. Eerdmans Publishing Co., 1956, p. 31.   (Italics not in original.)

. . . though Millennialism in one form or another can be traced back to the Apocalyptic literature prevalent among both Jews and Christians at the inception of the Christian movement, Dispensationalism is of recent origin and can boast a history of but little more than a hundred years.[6]

Philip Mauro recognized the divergence between dispensationalism and premillennialism when he asserted:

The entire system of dispensational thinking is modernistic in the strictest sense . . . . a system of doctrine that contradicts what has been held and taught by every Christian expositor from the beginning of the Christian era . . . suddenly made its appearance in the latter part of the nineteenth century.[7]

Failing to establish continuity between their account of the chronology of events surrounding the second coming of the Lord and the historic faith, dispensationalists attempt to find incipient seeds of their system in the natural distinctions involved in the varied usages of the words "Israel" and "Church," "Old Covenant" and "New Covenant," and "kingdom of God" and "kingdom of heaven" in the writing of various expositors of the Word in the history of the church. This approach is reflected in what Clarence Mason writes:

. . . It is a gratuitous assumption to suppose that dispensationalism was invented by Darby and his associates . . . . This writer submits that the dispensational viewpoint is inherent in the facts of the Bible's sequence of events . . . . It is relatively unimportant if one comes up with exactly seven. The argument of dispensationalism is sustained by a multiple-age dealing of God with man in His progressive self-revelation. Many of the early church believed and wrote about these various eras. They spoke of various ages. That none of them codified these ages specifically as dispensationalists do today does not deny that they could have been so codified. It is simply not true that there are only two covenants and thus two ages.[8]

In the same vein, Arnold Ehlert, who has compiled an extensive survey of the bibliographical data of dispensationalism, attempts to trace the presence of dispensational "systems" back,

6. John Wick Bowman, "The Bible and Modern Religions: II. Dispensationalism," *Interpretation,* 10:2:171 (April, 1956).

7. Philip Mauro, *The Gospel of the Kingdom.* Boston: Hamilton Bros., 1928, p. 9.

8. Clarence E. Mason, Jr., "A Review of 'Dispensationalism' by John Wick Bowman" (Part II), *Bibliotheca Sacra,* 114:1:15 (Jan.-Mar., 1957).

not only to apostolic times, but to Jewish and pre-Jewish thought. He details a list of more than a dozen "dispensationalism systems" that date back to two hundred years before Darby's time.[9]

What Ehlert does, however, and what Mason refers to in the passage just quoted, is nothing more than a recognition that various men have divided biblical history according to the natural divisions into which it falls. To recognize, as did William Cave (1637-1713), according to Ehlert's appraisal of his dispensational systems,[10] that biblical history may be divided into three areas: Patriarchical — from creation to Mount Sinai; Mosaical — from Sinai to the final period of the Jewish state; and Evangelical — to the end of the world, certainly does not establish the hermeneutical principle of contemporary dispensationalism.

Even the dispensationalism attributed to Pierre Poiret (1646-1719) does not follow the dispensationalism of today. The pattern of his thought is evident from the titles of his books: I. *The Oeconomy of the Creation;* II. *The Oeconomy of Sin;* III. *The Oeconomy of the Restoration before the Incarnation of Jesus Christ;* IV. *The Oeconomy of the Restoration after the Incarnation of Jesus Christ;* V. *The Oeconomy of the Cooperation of Man with the Operation of God;* and VI. *The Oeconomy of Universal Providence.*

Concerning Poiret's dispensationalism Ehlert writes:

> There is no question that we have here a genuine dispensational scheme. He uses the phrase "period or dispensation" and his seventh dispensation is a literal thousand-year millennium with Christ returned and reigning in bodily form upon the earth with His saints, and Israel regathered and converted![11]

The events cited in Poiret's dispensational system, however, neither vary from those to which the church has historically adhered, nor do they conform to the system of interpretation that is rooted in the theology of John Darby.

All of this illustrates a point that is often overlooked by many appraisers of this system who do not understand its

---

9. Arnold D. Ehlert, "A Bibliography of Dispensationalism," *Bibliotheca Sacra,* 101:1:95ff. (Jan.-Mar., 1944).

10. *Ibid.,* p. 448.

11. *Ibid.,* p. 449.

basic presupposition, and particularly by those who have grown up in it. The precise point is that the distinguishing features of dispensationalism do not involve merely a chronology of events about the end times, as important as this may be, but involve some basic principles of interpretation that depart radically from the historic Christian faith, and that are often diametrically opposed to what the church always believed.

The dispensationalism of John Darby and his followers is something different indeed from those attempts by theologians and biblical scholars of the past to understand God's relation to man as involving different periods of historical development of His revelation. No one will deny that the term "dispensation" is used in the Scriptures, nor that it was used in the history of theology prior to the nineteenth century. Both its use and meaning, however, have become significantly different since that time.

The line of continuity from Darby to the present can be traced unbroken from the works of his contemporaries: C. H. Mackintosh, William Trotter, William Kelly, and F. W. Grant, through the intermediary works of W. E. Blackstone, James Hall Brooks, A. J. Frost, G. Campbell Morgan,[12] Harry Ironside, A. C. Gaebelein, C. I. Scofield, and the Scofield

12. That the books written by Morgan and that his magnetic personal power from his important pulpit gave credence to dispensational teaching is beyond dispute. An interesting development in his views, however, for whatever accuracy it may have, is recorded in a letter by Paul G. Jackson published in the August 31, 1959, issue of *Christianity Today* (3:23:16-17), which is quoted here in part: "A dozen or more years before that date, during a Boston pastorate, I was privileged to attend a course of lectures given by Dr. Morgan at Gordon College. At the end of one session I ventured to ask: 'After your long study and extensive exposition of the Bible, Dr. Morgan, do you find any scriptural warrant for the distinction which many Bible teachers draw between the second coming of the Lord for his own (the rapture), and the coming of the Lord with his own (the revelation) with a time period of 3½ or 7 years between these two events?'

" 'Emphatically not!' Dr. Morgan replied. 'I know that view well, for in the earlier years of my ministry I taught it, and incorporated it in one of my books entitled *God's Method with Man*. But further study so convinced me of the error of this teaching that I actually went to the personal expense of buying the plates of that book from my own publisher and destroying them. The idea of a separate and secret coming of Christ to remove the church prior to his coming in power and glory is a vagary of prophetic interpretation without any Biblical basis whatsoever.' "

Bible,[13] to the contemporary adherents of his views. Gaebelein, who had the most influence on Scofield and who, through his works has probably done more to synthesize and promulgate dispensationalism than any other theologian, in referring to Darby writes: "I found in his writings, in the works of William Kelly, McIntosh, F. W. Grant, Bellett, and others the soul food I needed. I esteem these men next to the Apostles in their sound and spiritual teachings."[14] Speaking of the coming of the Lord, he ranks Darby among the leaders of the Christian faith. "What a meeting it will be! All the saints will be there . . . . No one will claim a denominational name or boast in a Cephas, a Paul, an Apollos, a Luther, or in the four Johns: John Calvin, John Knox, John Wesley, or John Darby."[15] The parallel between Scofield's notes and Darby's works only too clearly reveals that Scofield was not only a student of Darby's works, but that he copiously borrowed ideas, words, and phrases.

What, then, are the distinguishing features of dispensationalism? They are: its view of the nature and purpose of a dispensation; a rigidly applied literalism in the interpretation of Scripture; a dichotomy between Israel and the church; a restricted view of the church; a Jewish concept of the kingdom; a postponement of the kingdom; a distinction between law and grace that creates a multiple basis for God's dealing with man; a compartmentalization of Scripture; a pre-tribulation rapture; its view of the purpose of the great tribulation; its view of the nature of the millennial reign of Christ; its view of the eternal state, and its view of the apostate nature of Christendom.

All of these may be reduced to two basic features: dispensationalism is rooted in a hermeneutical principle of interpretation, and in a chronology of events that were not known in the historic faith of the church before its rise. To these

13. The pattern of the Scofield Bible is set by Darby's translation of the Bible, in which there are copious notes of "explanation" of the correct meaning of the passages. While Darby's is not organized as the Scofield Bible was later, the pattern is undoubtedly there.

14. A. C. Gaebelein, *Half a Century*. New York: Publication Office of *Our Hope*, 1930, p. 85. Here Gaebelein obviously means C. H. Mackintosh (CHM) though the name is misspelled.

15. *Ibid.*, p. 243.

may be added the tendency of dispensationalism to be separatistic in spirit and practice.

An analysis of these features is in order. They are not inclusive of all dispensational teaching, and undoubtedly overlap each other in some ways since they grow out of a common basis of interpretation. Furthermore, there are undoubtedly many who term themselves "dispensationalists" who would not agree that all of these features are a part of their theology. Nevertheless, *every* one of them is inherent in the system, and if all of the implications of the presuppositions of dispensationalism are pressed to their logical conclusions, all dispensationalists would be forced to accept them.

The paradox of the system lies precisely at this point: one cannot logically accept the *chronology* of dispensationalism without also accepting its basic principle of interpretation — that God works under different principles with mankind in different dispensations. It would be illogical, as an example, for one to accept the doctrine of the pretribulation rapture without also accepting the dispensational concept of the nature of the church, which has arisen out of its basic principle of interpretation. Once this basic principle has been accepted, the distinguishing features outlined here must logically also be accepted.

The Nature and Purpose of a Dispensation

Scofield defines a dispensation as "a period of time during which man is tested in respect of obedience to some specific revelation of the will of God."[16] He adds further: "These periods are marked off in Scripture by some *change* in God's method of dealing with mankind, in respect to two questions: of sin, and of man's responsibility. Each of the dispensations may be regarded as a new test of the natural man, and each ends in judgment — marking his utter failure in every dispensation."[17]

A dispensation is evidently a period of time in which God works with mankind in a different way than He does in another period of time. The College Standard Dictionary de-

16. C. I. Scofield, *Scofield Reference Bible*. New York: Oxford Univ. Press, 1917 edition, p. 5, fn. 4.
17. C. I. Scofield, *Rightly Dividing the Word of Truth*. Oakland: Western Book and Tract Co. n.d., p. 18, (Italics not in original.)

fines it as "the period during which a particular revelation of God's mind and will has been directly operative upon mankind, as during the Church dispensation."[18]

In formulating his dispensational divisions of the plan of God, Darby avers that

> the dispensations themselves all *declare some leading principles or interference of God, some condition in which He has placed man,* principles which in themselves are everlastingly sanctioned of God, but in the course of those dispensations placed responsibility in the hands of man for the display and discovery of what he was, and the bringing in their infallible establishment in Him to whom the glory of them all rightly belonged. It is not my intention to enter into any great detail, but to show simply how, *in every instance, there was a total and immediate failure as regarded man,* however the patience of God might tolerate and carry on by grace the dispensation in which man thus failed in the outset; and further, that *there is no instance of the restoration of a dispensation afforded us,* though there might be partial revivals of it through faith.[19]

Modern dispensationalism, based on Darby's earlier delineation of the principle of God's different relations to man, is best expressed by Lewis Sperry Chafer's statement that

> the Bible may be apportioned into well-defined periods. These periods are clearly separated and the recognition of their divisions *with their divine purposes* constitutes one of the most important factors in true interpretation of the Scriptures. These divisions of time are termed *dispensations* . . . . Man's relation to God is not the same in every age. It has been necessary to bring fallen man into divine testing . . . . Every dispensation, therefore, begins with man divinely placed in a *new* position of privilege and responsibility, and closes with the future of man resulting in righteous judgment from God. While there are certain abiding facts such as the holy character of God which are of necessity the same in every age, there are varying *instructions and responsibilities* which are, as to their application, limited to a given period . . . . A dispensation is more or less marked off by the new divine appointment and responsibilities with which it begins and by the divine judgments with which it ends.[20]

Nothing could be clearer than that dispensationalism views

18. The College Standard Dictionary, F. Vizetelly, ed. New York: Funk and Wagnalls Co., 1927, p. 339.

19. John Nelson Darby, *The Apostacy of the Successive Dispensations,* Col. Writ., Eccl. Vol. I, p. 193. (Italics not in original.)

20. Lewis Sperry Chafer, *Major Bible Themes.* Chicago: Moody Press, 1944, pp. 96-98. (Italics not in original.)

the continuous relation of God to man, from Adam to the present, as changing with each dispensation. God places man under different responsibilities, and conditions His action toward man according to each failure. William Trotter, one of the most active writers in the period when the incipient dispensationalism in Darby's thought was reaching its synthesis and systematization in the works of Scofield, and who had a pronounced influence upon Scofield, demonstrates this when he distinguishes the basis of dispensational division of God's relation to man thus:

> . . . in the gradual unfolding of God's purposes, dispensations have run, are running, and have yet to run their courses, so widely different in their character, that what is simple obedience and for the glory of God in one dispensation, may be entirely foreign to the character of another.[21]

Of such divisions and differentiated relations the historic Christian faith knows nothing. No such doctrine can be found in standard texts in any age of the history of the church. Samuel P. Tregelles, noted biblical scholar, textual critic, and one of the early Plymouth Brethren, in rejecting Darby's new interpretation termed it the "height of speculative nonsense."[22]

The Literal Interpretation of Scripture

There is something admirable about a system of interpretation that seeks to preserve the validity of the revealed Word of God, particularly if its validity is being questioned. The growth of dispensationalism paralleled the rise of a rationalistic attack upon the authority of the Bible. One great impetus to its growth has been an invariable insistence that the Bible must be taken literally as the Word of God, and its meaning must not be "spiritualized." To this day, in the minds of many, a non-literal interpretation is synonymous with liberalizing tendencies which are equated with denying the validity of the Word.

When the principle of literalness, however, is pressed in a rigid and unyielding manner upon every Scripture, this very principle, which is the natural one to be employed, actually

21. William Trotter, *Plain Papers on Prophetic Subjects.* New York: Loizeaux Bros., New Edition, Revised, n.d., p. 401.
22. Samuel P. Tregelles, as quoted in Charles E. Brown, *The Reign of Christ.* Anderson, Ind.: Gospel Trumpet Co., 1950, p. 54.

perverts the meaning of the text. Dispensationalism does this to the extreme.

Principles of interpretation are crucial for this or any other system of thought. The basic possible alternatives available to an interpreter may be summarized as follows:

> The different modes of interpreting the Bible which have generally obtained are . . . essentially the following three: the grammatical, the allegorical and the dogmatical. The grammatical mode of interpretation simply investigates the sense contained in the words of the Bible. The allegorical . . . maintains that the words of the Bible have, besides their simple sense, another which is concealed as behind a picture, and endeavors to find out this supposed figurative sense . . . . The dogmatical mode of interpretation endeavors to explain the Bible in harmony with the dogmas of the church. . . .[23]

Two basic principles of interpretation are thus available: the grammatical-historical (literal) and the allegorical. The literal method is that method which gives the word the meaning it would normally have according to its natural construction and usage. The allegorical method is that method which takes the same word and seeks to find a deeper meaning than the natural one. Both of these methods have been employed by biblical exegetes at every period of the history of the Christian church. "These two modes of interpretation, the allegorico-typical (literal) and the allegorico-mystical are found in the Christian writers as early as the first and second century."[24]

Dispensationalists insist, however, upon a rigid application of an exact literal interpretation, particularly as it has to do with Israel and the church. They insist on an unconditional literal fulfillment of all prophetic promises, failing to realize that by its very nature prophetic utterances are sometimes allegorical or symbolic.

An example of this unyielding attitude may be seen in this statement by John Walvoord, the acknowledged leader of academic dispensationalism, upon whose shoulders has fallen the mantle of Lewis Sperry Chafer.

> It is not difficult to prove from Scripture that Israel is frequently used in the New Testament to mean what it meant in the Old Testa-

23. John McClintoch and James Strong, editors, *Encyclopedia of Biblical, Theological and Ecclesiastical Literature,* "Interpretation," IV, 626.
24. *Ibid.*

ment — the nation descending from Abraham through Jacob. Further, *there is not a single reference in the New Testament to Israel which cannot be taken in its plain meaning. Not a single instance requires the term to include the Gentiles* . . . . There is no justification based on usage in the New Testament to interpret the word *Israel* as ever including Gentiles.[25]

Paul's assertion that "they are not all Israel, which are of Israel" (Rom. 9:6) would be difficult to explain if this principle were applied.

The most important consequence of dispensational literalism, however, is that it forces all *prophetic* Scripture into this rigidly defined pattern. This leads to exact futuristic fulfillment of every detail of early prophetic statements. The covenant with Abraham must be fulfilled in every *detail* to satisfy this principle of interpretation. It is obvious, however, that every detail is not to be literally fulfilled. Paul asserts in Galatians 3 that the promises were given to Abraham's seed, not "and unto seeds, as many; but as of one, and to thy seed, which is Christ" (3:16), and further "if ye be Christ's, then are ye [believers] Abraham's seed, and heirs according to the promise" (3:29). Surely the simple, natural, literal interpretation of these words indicates that there is at least a sense in which the promises to Abraham accrue to believers who, though not Jewish by natural descent, have nevertheless come to faith in Christ.

Out of such literalness comes a dichotomy between Israel and the church, so that there exists no parallel between the two. The universal and mediatorial kingdoms are two distinct entities; and the whole pattern of dispensational division follows.

If the pattern of rigid literalness is to be followed to its natural conclusions, the same dispensationalists who insist that the unconditional promises to Israel must be literally fulfilled as to the land, seat of government, restoration of temple, etc., during the millennial reign of Christ, must also (as true dispensationalists do) believe that the "new Jerusalem" described in the closing chapter of Revelation will actually be the eternal abode of the saints continuing on earth.

Dispensationalists will not interpret the obviously literal as literal, and the obviously symbolical as symbolical. Every-

25. John F. Walvoord, "Israel's Restoration," *Bibliotheca Sacra*, 103:4:409.

thing must be literal. R. C. H. Lenski, noted for his her-
meneutic scholarship, characterizes this type of interpretation
as follows:

> What is so depressing about the bulk of this exegesis . . . is its
> unexegetical character. Even words are not allowed to mean what
> they naturally and always mean. The presentations of the sound
> exegetes are ignored as though they did not exist. A sort of wilful
> resistance against what is even obvious pervades the majority.[26]

The purpose of this discussion, however, is not to refute the
principle of literal interpretation, but to reveal it, for whatever merit it may have, as a feature distinguishing dispensationalism from the church at all periods since its inception.
Actually, the method of literal interpretation is preferred by
this author, but is used with a natural recognition that some
Scripture is to be interpreted by its secondary or symbolical
meaning. That this has been the principle of interpretation
historically followed by the church, may easily be demonstrated
by a survey of theological literature, especially eschatological
literature, which contains none of the conclusions which have
grown out of dispensationalist literalism. This is not to
suggest that the church has not employed the literal grammatical-historical method, since it most certainly has. It has
not employed it so rigidly, however, as to deny the allegorical
where the allegorical is obviously meant, nor has it insisted
upon the literal where the literal was shown later to be allegorical, as in Galatians 3:16, 19.

LeRoy Froom's masterful survey of the history of eschatology
clearly demonstrates that until the nineteenth century the
church viewed Israel as having a place in the millennium, but
not as a separate entity, a different kingdom, as dispensational
literalism contends. Rather, Israel was viewed as a part of the
continual reign of Christ instituted in the church.[27]

The Dichotomy Between Israel and the Church

When the principle of rigid literalism is applied to the
promises of God to Abraham in instituting the nation of Israel,
two conclusions follow: God binds himself to fulfill every

26. R. C. H. Lenski, *The Interpretation of St. Paul's Epistle to the Romans.*
Columbus, Ohio: Lutheran Book Concern, 1936, p. 719.
27. LeRoy Edwin Froom, *The Prophetic Faith of Our Fathers.* Washington: Review and Herald, 1948.

promise to Israel exactly, and, since every detail of these covenants has not yet been fulfilled, Christ's future reign on earth will be for the purpose of fulfilling them in a relation to Israel *distinctly different from His present relation to the church.*

Herein lies another distinguishing feature of dispensationalism: that the whole of God's redemptive relation to man is centered in His covenantal relation to Israel. The implications of this division of God's redemptive relations are apparent: Israel, as a nation, is related to God by one principle (the unconditional covenant), while the church, as the body of Christ, is related to Him by an entirely different principle. The covenant is the key to the interpretation of all God's purposes in history, as Walvoord asserts:

> It is recognized by all serious students of the Bible that the Covenant with Abraham is one of the most important and determinative revelations of Scripture. It furnishes the key to the entire Old Testament and reaches for its fulfillment into the New. In the controversy between premillennialism [Walvoord here equates premillennialism with dispensationalism] and amillennialism the interpretation of this covenant more or less settles the entire argument. The analysis of its provision and the character of their fulfillment set the mold for the entire body of Scriptural truth.[28]

Chafer emphasizes the significance of the covenantal relation by asserting that "each covenant represents a divine purpose and the majority of them constitute an absolute prediction as well as an unalterable promise as the accomplishment of whatever God has designed."[29] He contends that in the one-covenant-of-grace idea "Scripture must be ignored or greatly misinterpreted to the end that such idealism may be advanced."[30] Furthermore, "to suppose that these two covenants — one for Israel and one for the Church — are the same is to assume that there is a latitude of common interest between God's purpose for Israel and His purpose for the Church."[31]

---

28. John F. Walvoord, "The Abraham Covenant and Pre-Millennialism," *Bibliotheca Sacra*, 108:4:414 (Oct.-Dec. 1951).

29. Chafer, *op. cit.*, p. 103. The "each covenant" and "majority of them" here refer to the Mosaic, Davidic, etc., reiteration of the basic covenant made with Abraham.

30. Lewis Sperry Chafer, *Systematic Theology*. Dallas: Dallas Seminary Press, 1948, II, 96.

31. *Ibid.*, p. 98.

This principle of covenantal relation clearly divides between Israel and the church as to their relation to God. It lays the groundwork for the dispensationalist concept of the church as being parenthetical to God's ongoing purposes for mankind. It separates God's relations into categories which are differentiated from each other by contrasting provisions, as Chafer graphically illustrates:

> Since all human life is lived under some *qualifying condition* belonging to the covenants of Jehovah, and since *every passage* of Scripture draws its color to some degree from the covenants *under which it belongs,* the importance to the Bible of a clear understanding of these age-characterizing, world-transforming declarations of Jehovah cannot be estimated.[32]

Such a concept is singularly missing from historic Christian theology. Whether it is a *good* principle of interpretation is left to the reader, but of its origin there can be little doubt: John Darby admits that it was a new truth that dawned upon him as a part of the development of his thought. Attributing it to a new revelation of God's plan, he writes, "The covenant is a word common in the language of a large class of Christian professors . . . but in its development and detail, as to its unfolded principles, much obscurity appears to me to have arisen from a want of simple attention to Scripture."[33]

In a letter written about the public reaction to his covenantal-relations doctrine, Darby wrote: ". . . I believe it to be the one true Scriptural ground of the church . . . ."[34] He added,

> I am daily more struck with the connection of the great principles on which my mind was exercised [during the period of his salvation and the genesis of his theology] . . . . Christ coming to receive us to Himself: and collaterally with that, the setting up of a new earthly dispensation, from Isaiah XXXII . . . . It was a vague fact that received form in my mind long after, that there must be a wholly new order of things . . . .[35]

Darby is pointedly correct in stating that this came to him as a new truth, since it is not to be found in theological liter-

32. Chafer, *Major Bible Themes,* p. 104. (Italics not in original.)
33. J. N. Darby, *The Covenants,* Col. Writ., Doc. Vol. I, p. 68.
34. J. N. Darby, *Letters of J. N. D.,* I, 343.
35. *Ibid.,* pp. 344-345.

ature prior to his proclamation of it.[36] It is not that exegetes prior to his time did not see a covenant between God and Israel, or a future relation of Israel to the millennial reign, but they always viewed the church as a continuation of God's single program of redemption begun in Israel. It is dispensationalism's rigid insistence on a distinct cleavage between Israel and the church, and its belief in a later unconditional fulfillment of the Abrahamic covenant, that sets it off from the historic faith of the church.

> Now surely, as commentators of all times have clearly pointed out, especially already Luther and Calvin, this promise to Israel is conditional, requiring faith . . . . History is the best commentary on how the promise is meant. When the Jews definitely cast off Christ, they were definitely as a nation expelled from the land. All who fall back upon this promise as guaranteeing a restoration of Palestine to the Jews . . . have laid into it a meaning which the words simply do not carry.[37]

A Restricted View of the Church

The most paradoxical aspect of dispensationalism is its view of the church. Modern dispensationalism insists that the church is an "interruption" of God's plan with Israel necessitated by the rejection of the kingdom by the Jews when it was offered to them by Jesus. This idea was most certainly fathered by John Darby — it is at the very heart of his theology — yet he maintained a very "spiritual" concept of the church "in the heavenlies." He insisted that the church, now the body of Christ, the habitation of God, is, nevertheless, distinctly not a part of God's initial redemptive plan.

Raymond Ohman accurately presents the dispensational restricted view of the church:

> . . . the coming Millennium articulates not with the Church age but rather with the dispensation of law . . . the kingdom age follows

---

36. The reader must be reminded that Darby did not develop his thought in a theological vacuum. When the author attributes an idea to Darby, as above, he does not mean to imply that Darby originated it alone, since he most certainly was influenced by others. Darby's dependence upon the Irvingites, upon the concepts of Rebald and others, must be acknowledged. When a view is attributed here to Darby it implies that he developed and promoted it, if he did not actually originate it alone.

37. H. C. Leupold, *Exposition of Genesis.* Columbus: Wartburg Press, 1942, p. 490.

> as if it comes immediately after the Old Testament and the kingdom
> promises of the Gospel [as if the Church never existed].[38]

In describing the place of the church in the total redemptive
scheme, Harry Ironside called it a parenthesis. Chafer accepts
the principles involved here — that the church has no connection with God's previous acts in history, and a subordinate
role — but widens the gulf even further when he asserts:

> The new, hitherto unrevealed purpose of God in the outcalling of a
> heavenly people from Jews and Gentiles is so divergent with respect
> to the divine purpose toward Israel, which purpose preceded it and
> will yet follow it, that the term *parenthetical,* commonly employed
> to describe the new age-purpose, is inaccurate. A parenthetical
> portion sustains some direct or indirect relation to that which goes
> before or that which follows after: *but the present age-purpose is
> not thus related* and therefore is more properly termed an *intercala-
> tion.* The appropriateness of this word will be seen in the fact
> that as an interpolation is formed by inserting a word or phrase into
> a context, so an intercalation is formed by introducing a day or
> period of time into a calendar.[39]

The contrast is stated even more definitely by C. I. Scofield:

> Looking then for the birth of the church we find *(contrary, perhaps,
> to our expectations, for we have probably been taught that Adam and
> the patriarchs are in the Church)* that it certainly did not exist
> before or during the earth-life of Christ . . . . Scripturally we find
> the birth of the Church in Acts II and the termination of its career
> on earth in I Thess. IV. Comparing then, what is said in Scripture
> concerning Israel and the Church, we find that in origin, calling,
> promise, worship, principles of conduct and future destiny all is
> contrast.
> . . . In the predictions concerning the future of Israel and the Church
> the distincion is still more startling. The Church will be taken
> away from the earth entirely, but restored. Israel is yet to have
> her greatest splendor and power . . . . Thus it is seen that the
> elementary distinction between Israel and the Church is that the
> former is of and for the earth, the latter of and for heaven; the
> former is under a covenant of works, the latter the object of
> unconditional grace.[40]

38. Raymond N. Ohman, "The Biblical Doctrine of the Millennium."
Unpublished Doctoral Dissertation, Dallas Theological Seminary, Dallas,
Texas, 1949, p. 149.

39. Chafer, *Systematic Theology,* IV, 41.

40. C. I. Scofield, *Scofield Bible Correspondence Course.* Chicago: Moody
Bible Institute, 19th edition, pp. 23-25.

Again, historic Christianity has not denied that there are certain differences between Israel and the church. It certainly has not, however, made the differences as dialectically distinct as does dispensationalism. The view that has prevailed among historic premillennialists is that the Cross amalgamates the Jew and Gentile into one group standing before God in need of grace. It has interpreted Paul's statement that there is neither Jew nor Greek to mean that all have the same relation in grace before God. Admittedly, premillennialists have seen that Israel as a nation would have some relation to the millennium, but this relation is not totally separated in basis or purpose from that of the body of Christ regenerated in grace.

The church has been viewed as the natural development of God's plan, not as a parenthesis or an intercalation — not as an entity aside from God's main redemptive stream. Admittedly dispensationalism views the church as the Bride of Christ, and thus holds it in high esteem. Nevertheless, by separating it from the total redemptive plan begun in Adam, dispensationalism restricts the role of the church far more than does the historic view.

A Jewish Concept of the Kingdom

Premillennialists have always believed that there is to be a future kingdom in which Christ would physically reign on earth. This kingdom is to be the cataclysmic consummation of God's redemptive reign, ushered in by the visible, personal, literal return of Christ before the millennium.

Dispensationalism, however, restricts the future kingdom to a restoration of the Jewish kingdom which supposedly was offered to the Jews by Christ, but which they rejected, and on which basis the church was instituted. The assertion that the kingdom which Christ offered was not a spiritual kingdom, but a literal fulfillment of the Abrahamic promises is basic to this view. As A. C. Gaebelein puts it,

> What then is the Gospel of the Kingdom? As we learn in the beginning of the Gospel of Matthew, the Gospel of the Kingdom is the good news that the promised Kingdom of the Old Testament was about to be established with the manifestation of the King.[41]

The historic interpretation has been that Jesus offered a

41. A. C. Gaebelein, *The Gospel of Matthew*. New York: Our Hope Press, 1909, II, 189.

spiritual kingdom, and for that reason it was rejected. Had Jesus offered an actual restoration of the throne of David to the Jews of his day he undoubtedly would have been accepted. Since the kingdom was rejected by Israel, avows historic pre-millennialism, the "spiritual" Israel in the form of the church was instituted, and finds its consummation in the millennial kingdom. The church is viewed as the recipient of the covenantal relation with God, the transfer being sealed by the death and resurrection of Christ. The church, therefore, is the epitome of God's redemptive plan, since it is in the church that Christ is said to reign.

Adhering to its rigid literalism and unconditional covenant, dispensationalism, however, insists that the church in no wise assumes any of Israel's relation to God; that there can be no "spiritual Israel"; and that the promises of the Abrahamic covenant are still inviolate.

> The nation to whom the Lord promises the Kingdom is not the Church. The church is called the Body of Christ, the Bride of Christ, the Habitation of God by the Spirit, the Lamb's wife, but never a nation. The nation is Israel still, but that believing remnant of the nation, living when the Lord comes.[42]

A sharp distinction is made by dispensationalism, not only between the kingdom and the church, but between the gospels which were preached to each. The gospel Jesus preached was of the kingdom. The gospel of grace was not preached until the church was instituted, when it was revealed to Paul. J. Dwight Pentecost, one of the leading academic dispensationalists, illustrates this separation in an extreme form:

> It is quite evident that this Gospel of the Kingdom required personal acceptance on the part of the hearers. Christ, talking to Nicodemus proclaiming the gospel of the Kingdom, said, Except one be born anew, he cannot see the kingdom of God [John 3:3].[43]

The apparent implication here is that Nicodemus would have been "born anew" into the kingdom then to be instituted, not into the same kingdom into which men are born today when they exercise faith in the resurrected Christ.

---

42. A. C. Gaebelein, *Hath God Cast Away His People?* New York: Gospel Publishing House, 1905, p. 158. Gaebelein apparently overlooked I Peter 2:9 where the church is called a "holy nation."

43. J. Dwight Pentecost, "The Judgment of the Nation." Unpublished Master's Thesis, Dallas Theological Seminary, Dallas, Texas, 1941, p. 48.

Dispensationalists see a difference between the kingdom of God and the kingdom of heaven. The kingdom of God is the universal sovereign reign of God in the hearts of men, while the kingdom of heaven is an earthly rule of God. Chafer describes the kingdom of heaven as: *theocratic,* in the time of the patriarchs; *covenanted,* with Israel; *predicted,* in its prophetic anticipation; *announced,* through John the Baptist, Christ, and later by the Apostles, but *rejected; postponed,* until the second advent; now in *mystery;* and finally to be *realized* when Christ will offer again to Israel the same kingdom He offered in the first advent, which this time will be accepted.[44]

On this basis, the kingdom which is to be instituted in the millennial reign will be distinctly Jewish, with the land occupied, the throne of David established again, the temple restored and even the sacrifices re-instituted: all of this with no relation whatsoever to what has been established in the church and through the death of Christ.

No part of historic Christian doctrine supports this radical distinction between church and kingdom. To be sure, they are not identical; but dispensationalism has added the idea that the kingdom was to be a restoration of Israel, not a consummation of the church. James Bear poignantly indicates the difference between this teaching and historic premillennialism in these words:

> Both believed in a Kingdom of Christ on earth after His Return. But the historic pre-millennialist exalted the Church and held that the Church enjoyed the Kingdom. If the Jews were to have any place of preeminence, it was because of their Christian zeal. If they were to enjoy the Kingdom, it was because they had become a part of the Church.
>
> Modern Pre-millennialists, following the Dispensational lead, make the Kingdom a Jewish Kingdom, given to the Jews because they are Jews. The Church has become a special group different in character and destiny from those who enjoy the Kingdom.[45]

The Postponed Kingdom

The idea of the postponed kingdom is inherent in the Jewish concept of the kingdom discussed above, and is delineated here

44. Chafer, *Systematic Theology,* IV, 224.
45. James E. Bear, "Historic Premillennialism," *Union Seminary Review*: Richmond, Union Theological Seminary. 55:2:219 (May, 1944).

only to set it apart as a definite feature of dispensationalism which distinguishes it from the historic faith.

The postponed-kingdom idea grows out of the basic concept of what the kingdom was to be, and what it shall yet be. This is held to be a literal restoration of the national kingdom, and since no such covenanted kingdom with the Davidic throne has appeared, it must have been postponed. The kingdom and the church can in no way be paralleled in the plan of God.

C. L. Feinberg summarizes this point well.[46] There had been a promise that David would have a man to sit on his throne, but Israel had not seen this heir. Then the King comes. He offers the kingdom to the Jews, without needing to explain what the kingdom is. Such explanation would have been pointless, since the Jews had the Old Testament expectation of the Davidic kingdom. National repentance was the condition on which the kingdom was to be instituted, but Israel did not repent — it rejected its King. However, the promise of the kingdom had not been conditioned on their acceptance, so their rejection did not nullify the promise. Hence the church was instituted as the "mystery" form of the kingdom, but in no sense the fulfillment of it. Israel had seemingly lost the kingdom.

> But God's plans are not so easily and lightly disposed of. Shall all the multiplied promises of God of the Old Testament that involve His faithfulness and everlasting divine holiness . . . with relation to the covenanted and prophesied kingdom of the Son of David be forever unrealized? . . . In the resurrected King, then, would all the covenanted promises have to be fulfilled.
>
> The kingdom that was to be instituted was recognized as having a beginning in the kingdom of David, of whose seed Jesus Christ was made according to the flesh . . . the kingdom yet future will be the Davidic kingdom, ruled over by the Son of David.
>
> . . . the restoration referred to is that of the kingdom to Israel . . . .[47]

Some dispensationalists object to the use of the term "postponement" because it suggests a change in God's plan. Van Ryan presents this view:

> . . . the kingdom was offered in order to set in motion the plan long before conceived in heaven in the courts of Deity. Here in-

46. Charles L. Feinberg, *Premillennialism or Amillennialism*. Wheaton, Ill.: Van Kampen Press, 1954, pp. 59ff.

47. *Ibid.*, pp. 76, 75.

deed all went accordng to plan. No change, no postponement, but all is simple and natural in its order. No "If" has any place here.[48]

Walvoord concurs in this emphasis by stating, "Our position is that Christ came to *offer* the kingdom, not actually set it up."[49] While both of these statements avoid the connotation of a changed plan necessitated by Israel's rejection, at the same time they emphatically affirm the very idea that distinguishes this concept — that the Church in no wise is a part of the redemptive plan of God which was begun in Israel, and that the primary purpose of the future millennial reign is to be the literal fulfillment of the Abrahamic and Davidic covenants.

Such an extreme emphasis on the "postponed" kingdom, or even the "offered, but not set up" kingdom ultimately detracts from the glory of the church, which glory stems from the crucified and resurrected Christ. An emphasis upon the national restoration of Israel is, at the same time, a de-emphasis upon the triumph of the cross, by which believers are made members of the body of Christ, the church.

Premillennialists have always believed that Israel would have a relation to God in the millennium, but this relation is established by grace through the death of Christ. The historic faith has held that the kingdom was not postponed, but fulfilled in the church, and will come to its consummation in the millennial reign — all on the basis of the resurrected Christ. Dispensationalism contends that when Israel rejected Christ nationally it rejected only the *privilege, opportunity,* and *blessings* of the kingdom; while historic premillennialism contends that Israel nationally rejected the *basis* upon which they were to be established — Christ, the Lord. If, therefore, Israel is to be restored, it will be restored only when it accepts the *basis* of the kingdom, salvation through grace.

The Distinction Between Law and Grace, Creating a Multiple Basis for God's Dealing with Man

Perhaps no presupposition of dispensationalism will be denied more vigorously than this one. Certainly most pastors who adhere in general to dispensationalism will not admit

48. August Van Ryan, *The Kingdom of God and of Heaven.* New York: Loizeaux Bros., 1946, p. 20.

49. Walvoord, as quoted by Harley E. Rowe, "The Kingdom in Matthew," Unpublished Master's Thesis, Dallas Theological Seminary, 1955, p. 15.

that they believe this. Nevertheless, the presupposition of the difference between law and grace, between Israel and the church, between the different relations of God to men in the different dispensations, when carried to its logical conclusion will inevitably result in a multiple form of salvation — that men are not saved the same way in all ages.

Undoubtedly dispensationalists do contend that God acts *graciously* toward men in all dispensations, since all of God's acts are gracious. There is a difference, however, between saying that God acts graciously toward men and saying that men are saved by grace through the death of Christ. Two things are significant here: the distinction between law and grace, and its implications concerning the basis of salvation.

The distinction between law and grace is described in the Scofield Bible as follows:

> Grace . . . is, therefore, constantly set in contrast to law, under which God demands righteousness from man, as, under grace he gives righteousness to man. Law is connected with Moses and works; grace with Christ and faith.
>
> As a dispensation grace begins with the death and resurrection of Christ. The point of testing is no longer *legal obedience,* but acceptance or rejection of Christ . . . .[50]

Chafer adds to this definition that "according to the Scripture [the law] with its covenant of works is the one principle which is opposed to the teaching of grace."[51] Scofield further contrasts the two:

> The most obvious and striking division of the word of truth is that between law and grace. Indeed, these contrasting principles characterize the two most important dispensations — the Jewish and Christian.
>
> The key word to all inspired writings from Ex. XX:1 to Mal. IV:6 is law.
>
> The key word to all the inspired writings from the narrative of the crucifixion in the Gospels to the end of Revelation is grace. The four Gospels have an intermediate character.
>
> It is . . . of the most vital moment to observe that Scripture never, in *any* dispensation, *mingles* these two principles . . . . Everywhere the Scriptures present law and grace in sharply contrasted spheres.[52]

50. Scofield, *Scofield Reference Bible,* p. 1115, fn. 1, 2.
51. Lewis Sperry Chafer, *Grace,* Chicago: Moody Press, 1945, p. 102.
52. Scofield, *Scofield Bible Correspondence Course,* pp. 27-28. (Italics in original.)

This distinction implies that there are two principles under which man has been saved — law and grace. Dispensationalists, of course, will deny this. Chafer, in the context cited above, adds, "The law was never given as a means of salvation or justification . . ."[53] and in another work, "The sinner is saved in every age by grace."[54] Raymond Ohman also asserts:

> The millennialist . . . sees the universal necessity for and efficacy of the death of Christ as to salvation. This does not alter the fact that God's dealing with his people may be different in one dispensation from His dealing with His people in another dispensation . . . . However God may seek to move a people or may seek to apply His salvation has nothing to do with the one way of salvation through the work of Christ . . . .[55]

However, these assertions of a single principle of salvation simply contradict the basic ideas of the system. Its protestations to the contrary, dispensationalism has constructed a system in which law and grace work against each other, not conjointly. In spite of his assertion that men are always saved by grace, Chafer's system of interpretation insists that "with the call of Abraham and the giving of the Law . . . there are two widely different, standardized, divine provisions whereby man, who is utterly fallen, might come into the favor of God.[56]
The very concept of the dispensations involves this difference. If a dispensation is a "period of time during which man is being tested in respect of obedience to some specific revelation of his will" and if "these periods are marked by some change in God's method of dealing with mankind," and if "each dispensation ends in judgment, making utter failure of that method," the logical conclusion is that God must be dealing with man in terms of different principles in different periods. John Darby underscores this conclusion by referring to the error "of confounding the law and the gospel, the past economics or dispensations with the present one."[57] Harry A. Ironside definitely had this in mind when he defined a dispensation as a "period of time . . . in which God is dealing

53. Chafer, *op. cit.*, p. 113.
54. Chafer, *Systematic Theology*, IV, 181.
55. Ohman, *op. cit.*, pp. 141, 142.
56. Lewis Sperry Chafer, "Dispensationalism," *Bibliotheca Sacra*, 93:4:410.
57. Darby, *The Hopes of the Church of God in Connection With the Destiny of the Jews and the Nations, as Revealed in Prophecy*. Col. Writ., Pro. Vol. I, p. 564.

with men in a different way than He has ever dealt with them before."[58]

Dispensationalism contains not only an inherent multiple basis of salvation in the past, but in the future as well. There is little doubt as to this dispensational stand. J. Dwight Pentecost affirms, for instance:

> This is not the Gospel of Grace, but rather the good news of the kingdom. *This Gospel of the Kingdom is not being preached now*, for after the final rejection of the Kingship of Christ by the Jews, at the stoning of Stephen, God called another man, Paul, and revealed to him the Gospel of Grace. When God will have completed the body of Christ, and will have taken them to be with Himself at the rapture, when the return of Christ in power and glory draws nigh, then . . . *the gospel of the kingdom will be preached* in all the world for a witness unto all nations.[59]

W. B. Riley has the same idea: Christ, he says, used language with precision. When He said "this gospel of the kingdom" He did not mean "this gospel of grace" or "this gospel of personal salvation," but specifically the "kingdom gospel."[60] Thorough understanding must be achieved at this point. Dispensationalists do insist that there is no multiple basis of salvation in their system. It is legitimate to ask, however, whether their own system of interpretation does not protest strongly against them. If one were to take seriously the dichotomies involved here — Israel-church, church-kingdom, gospel of the kingdom — gospel of grace, etc. — would one not conclude, in spite of protest to the contrary, that multiple basis is inevitable for one who orients his theology in this system?

Even if one takes seriously the dispensationalists' denial of a multiple basis of salvation, he may legitimately question their concept of two "gospels" on both scriptural and historical grounds. According to the Apostle Paul in Galatians 1:6, 7, there is only one gospel, the gospel of grace. And the testimony of history shows that the church never separated law and grace, or the gospel now and the gospel of the future, in the way described by dispensationalism.

58. Harry A. Ironside, *The Lamp of Prophecy*. Grand Rapids: Zondervan, 1940, p. 43.
59. Pentecost, *Judgments*, p. 49.   (Italics not in original.)
60. W. B. Riley, *The Evolution of the Kingdom*. New York: Charles C. Cook, 1913, p. 157.

The Compartmentalization of Scripture

Dispensationalism divides Scripture according to classes of people, insisting that no single passage can have primary application to two dispensations at the same time. While many nominal dispensationalists undoubtedly do not realize it, this is an inevitable conclusion of their system.

Chafer establishes this point by laying down as a fundamental principle for interpreting the Bible that:

> . . . the Bible student must recognize the difference between a primary and a secondary application of the Word of God. Only those portions of the Scriptures which are directly addressed to the child of God under grace are to be given a personal or primary application . . . . it does not follow that the Chistian is appointed by God to conform to those governing principles which were the will of God for people of other dispensations.
>
> Since the child of God depends wholly on the instructions contained in the Bible for his direction in daily life, and since the principles obtaining in the various dispensations are so diverse, and at times even contradictory, it is important that they shall recognize those portions of the Scriptures which directly apply to him. . . . It is obvious that, apart from the knowledge of dispensational truth, the believer will not be intelligently adjusted to the present purpose and will of God in the world. Such knowledge alone will save him from assuming the hopeless legality of the dispensation that is past or from undertaking the impossible world-transforming program belonging to the dispensation which is to come.[61]

Though this principle could be drawn from practically every writer on dispensational "truth," I. M. Haldeman's statement will suffice to illustrate the point further:

> To confound these dispensations, to take the principle of action revealed in one and apply it indiscriminately to another, to ignore the classes of persons and the peculiar aims of each dispensation is to produce confusion, contradiction and lay foundations for that disharmony which reigns all too manifestly today among Christian expositors. . . . We have no right to take truth from one class and give it to another. . . . Whole sections, chapters, and passages have been taken bodily from the Jew and transferred without compunction to the Church and Christians.[62]

The implications here are apparent — certain parts of the Bible may be restricted to certain people, and entire groups

61. Chafer, *Major Bible Themes*, pp. 97-98.

62. I. M. Haldeman, *How to Study the Bible*. New York: Charles C. Cook, 1904, pp. 7, 3.

may be exempt from others. If, as dispensationalism avows, the church was not instituted until Pentecost, none of the Gospels apply directly to the Christian: the sermon on the mount, the Lord's Prayer, the ethical teaching of Jesus — these all are "kingdom truths." Even after Pentecost the kingdom was offered again by Peter, and even a third time at the stoning of Stephen; hence the Book of Acts must then be divided between those passages referring to the Jew and kingdom and those referring to Gentile and church.

No further word need be added. Such a divisive compartmentalizing of the Scriptures speaks for itself. While it is an inherent part of the dispensational system, it has not been a part of the historic Christian faith or even of historic premillennialism. Since the canonization of the New Testament, a unitary view of the Bible has been the guiding principle of interpretation for the church. A continuity in the message of the Scriptures has been accepted as the basis for understanding it. Dispensational compartmentalization is a departure from the historic faith.

The Pre-Tribulation Rapture

Undoubtedly the point at which most people accept dispensationalism is in the doctrine of the rapture of the church before the great tribulation. Unknowingly, many identify this as the only premillennial position, although in the entire history of prophetic interpretation this idea is unknown. Premillennialists have always believed that Christ would return personally, literally, and visibly to establish the millennial reign, but only with the advent of dispensationalism has the pre-tribulation concept emerged.

Many reasons are usually cited for the necessity of the pre-tribulation rapture. Exegetically, the interpretation of I Thessalonians 4:16-17 is given, "For the Lord himself shall descend from heaven with a shout, with the voice of the archangel, and with the trump of God: and the dead in Christ shall rise first: Then we which are alive shall be caught up together with them in the clouds, to meet the Lord in the air: and so shall we ever be with the Lord." This verse says nothing, however, about rapture in the dispensational sense. It pointedly does not say that the church will be taken out of the world, only to return at a later time. Only when this verse is fitted into the general dispensational scheme, and joined to other verses, can it be given this meaning. Only by involved exegetical interpretation can the pre-tribulation rapture be supported.

This precisely demonstrates one of the characteristic features of dispensationalism. The idea of rapture does not arise from exegesis, even for dispensationalism, but from its concept of the church. This fact is emphasized by Walvoord:

> In determining the question of whether the Church will go through the tribulation, a most important factor is the definition of the term Church . . . . It is therefore not too much to say that the rapture question is determined more by ecclesiology than eschatology . . . . Any answer to the rapture question must therefore be based upon a careful study of the doctrine of the Church as it is revealed in the New Testament.[63]

The doctrine of the church to which Walvoord refers grows out of Darby's doctrine, which views the basis of the church in its "heavenly existence," not its earthly form:

> Those who believe in the rapture of the Church before the appearing of Christ hold that the Church has a special and peculiar character and connection with Christ . . . . The Church's joining Christ has nothing to do with Christ's appearing or coming to earth. Her place is elsewhere. She sits in Him *already* in heavenly places. She has to be brought there as to bodily presence . . . . The thing she has to expect for herself is not . . . Christ's appearing, but her being taken up where He is . . . . *It is this conviction, that the Church is properly heavenly, in its calling and relationship with Christ, forming no part of the course of events of the earth, which makes the rapture so simple and clear: and on the other hand, it shows how the denial of its rapture brings down the Church to an earthly position, and destroys its whole spiritual character and position.*[64]

The Old Testament saints are excluded from the church:

> It may therefore be concluded . . . that the believers in the present age are quite distinct from either the believer of the Old Testament or believers of future ages.

---

63. John F. Walvoord, *The Rapture Question.* Findlay, Ohio: Dunham Publ. Co., 1957, pp. 15-16.

64. J. N. Darby, *"The Rapture of the Saints,"* Col. Writ., Pro. Vol. IV, pp. 180, 233, 237. (Italics not in original.) If this position were pressed to its logical conclusions it would assert that not the *coming of the Lord* is the blessed hope of the church, but rather the raptured *going of the church.*

. . . the conclusion is clearly drawn that the body of believers in the present age which composes the Church has a distinct place in God's plan and program and as such is contrasted to saints who will come to know Christ in the tribulation period or in the future millennium.[65]

The pre-tribulation rapture view is, of course, rooted in the principle of interpretation which separates the church from the total redemptive plan of God. The church must be raptured out of the world before the tribulation because it is not a part of the kingdom, which will be in its inital stage of restoration through the remnant that survives the tribulation.

Darby himself admitted the novelty of his teaching when he wrote:

> The rapture of the saints to meet the Lord in the air, before His manifestation to the earth, and the existence of a Jewish remnant in whom the Spirit of God is graciously working before the Lord manifests Himself to them for their deliverance, is happily attracting the attention of Christians. It has made sufficient way to be the occasion of renewed opposition . . . .[66]

One does not wonder that the pre-tribulation rapture brought opposition, since it was contrary to what the best of historic premillennial scholarship had taught. This point is so important that it needs careful documentation. Alexander Reese, in attempting to establish its discontinuity with the historic faith, lists an imposing array of great biblical scholars since apostolic time who, though premillennialists, have not interpreted the New Testament as teaching a separate rapture.[67] This is understandable since, without the basic

65. Walvoord, *op. cit.*, pp. 34, 38.

66. Darby, *op. cit.*, p. 179.

67. Alexander Reese, *The Approaching Advent of Christ*. London: Marshall, Morgan & Scott, Ltd., n.d., pp. 18, 19. Among those mentioned are Irenaeus, Tertullian, Justin Martyr, Mede, Bengel, Alford, Ellicott, Moorehead, Müller, Maitland, Saphir, Tregelles, Trench, West, Delitzsch, Ebard, Godet, Lange, Van Oosterzee, and Zahn, all of whom have been noted for their careful scholarship and great contributions to the historic faith. For further study he suggests C. D. Maitland's *Apostolic School of Prophetic Interpretation* and Nathaniel West's *Thousand Years in Both Testaments* and *Premillennial Essays of the Prophetic Conferences,* to which I add D. T. Taylor's, *The Voice of the Church on the Coming and Kingdom of the Redeemer,* LeRoy Froom's *The Prophetic Faith of Our Fathers,* and an excellent article by C. A. Briggs on "The Origin and

presupposition of the absolute dichotomy between Israel and the church, the verses referring to the church's being "caught up" simply cannot be interpreted to teach the dispensational rapture. Reese concludes by stating:

> About 1830, however, a new school arose within the fold of pre-millennialism that sought to overthrow what, since the Apostolic Age, have been considered by all pre-millennialists as established results, and to institute in their place a series of doctrines that had never been heard of before. The school . . . is founded by J. N. Darby.[68]

Even dispensationalists admit the late development of this doctrine. Walvoord admits, "This teaching was espoused of Darby and the Plymouth Brethren and popularized by the famous Scofiled Bible," and later refers to the "detailed development of pre-tribulation truth during the past few centuries."[69] Ironside, in writing about the Powerscourt Prophetic conferences (of which Darby was the leader) states, "It was in these meetings that the precious truth of the rapture of the Church was brought to light."[70]

The Purpose of the Great Tribulation

Belief in *a* tribulation as taught in Jeremiah 30, Daniel 12, Matthew 24, and Revelation 7, has also been a characteristic of historic premillennialism. The question in point, however, is the purpose of this tribulation. Historic premillenialism knows nothing of the *Great Tribulation,* which according to dispensationalism has a special purpose relating to the Jewish kingdom.

> The Scriptures teach plainly . . . that in sharp contrast to general tribulation, which all may expect, a future period of unprecedented tribulation is in prospect which will overshadow and be distinct from all previous times of trouble. This future time of trouble . . . will concern three classes of people: (1) the nation Israel; (2) the pagan Gentile world; (3) the saints or elect who will live in that

History of Premillennialism" in the *Lutheran Quarterly,* 9:2:207-245 (1879). All of these amply support the contention that of the pretribulation rapture before the advent of dispensationalism, the historic faith knew nothing!

68. *Loc. cit.*

69. Walvoord, *op. cit.,* p. 5.

70. Harry A. Ironside, *A Historical Sketch of the Brethren Movement.* Grand Rapids: Zondervan, 1942, p. 23.

time of trouble. It is of utmost significance that every Scripture
which describes the participants in this future tribulation period
refers to Israelites as Israelites, Gentiles as Gentiles, and saints
as saints without ever once using any of the distinctive terms that
apply to believers in this present age.[71]

Following the chronological chart of events developed by
dispensationalists such as Clarence Larkin[72] and W. E. Blackstone,[73] G. D. Beckwith summarizes the events of the Great
Tribulation substantially as follows.[74]

The church is removed from the earth in the rapture; the
seven-year period which follows is divided into two three-and-
one-half-year periods, during the first of which Israel enters
into a covenant with the antichrist, who breaks it at the end.
The second half-period begins when Satan overpowers the
antichrist and the "time of Jacob's trouble" is poured out on
the world. During the seven years of tribulation the gospel of
the kingdom (notice: *not* the gospel of grace) is preached. An
elect remnant of Israel, numbering 144,000, survives the tribulation to become the kingdom to which Christ returns after
the seven years.

The basis for teaching such a tribulation is the over-all
system of dispensationalism, rooted in the ever present distinction between Israel and the church. The pre-tribulation rapture grows out of this concept, since the church must be
removed before the remnant of Israel is gathered. The dichotomy between law and grace as multiple ways of divine dealing
with man also lies behind this concept. Beckwith illustrates
what must be the inevitable conclusion of this method of
interpretation when he says of the petition "Thy kingdom
come" in the Lord's Prayer: "In the prayer Jesus taught His
disciples . . . they prayed for the real kingdom of Christ which
follows the tribulation period and the Revelation of Christ."[75]

71. Walvoord, *op. cit.*, p. 43. The saints mentioned here are not to
be confused with the church which, according to dispensationalism, will
have been raptured out of the world.

72. Clarence Larkin, *Dispensational Truths*. Philadelphia: Published by
the author, 1920.

73. W. E. Blackstone, *Jesus is Coming*. New York: Fleming H. Revell,
1908.

74. George D. Beckwith, *God's Prophetic Plan*. Grand Rapids: Zondervan, 1942, pp. 98ff.

75. *Ibid.*, p. 100.

Since the concept of the Great Tribulation grows out of the dispensational principle of interpretation, and since this principle is unknown in the historic faith of the church, it follows naturally that this concept is also new. What has been previously written in documentation of the pre-tribulation rapture view applies equally here.

The Nature of the Millennial Reign of Christ

It is not an understatement to say that dispensationalism focuses chiefly on the millennium. Since the church is paren-thetical, or at least intercalational, and since the kingdom was promised to Abraham, reconfirmed in David, and offered but not accepted in Christ, the entire consummation of God's plan for Israel is epitomized in the restored kingdom to be established by Christ in the millennium.

It will be seen at once that the dispensationalist millennium is decidedly Jewish in character. Regathered Israel will be the focus of Christ's activity.

> The millennium is that period of one thousand years, prophesied in the Scriptures, of the personal, world-wide, glorious reign of the Son of David our Lord Jesus Christ, who after His literal return from heaven will fulfill in the earth the promises made to Abraham, Isaac and Jacob, to restore Israel to her own land, and to give her the realization of God's covenant promises . . . .[76]
> "Come, ye blessed of my Father, inherit the kingdom prepared for you from the foundation of the world" (Matt. 25:34). It is recognized that this kingdom prepared from the foundation of the world is the earthly Messianic kingdom prepared for Israel, the hope promised to every true Israelite.[77]

The millennium is to be a literal fulfillment of Old Testament prophecy; therefore its government will be theocratic. Christ will have a physical throne upon which He sits to rule over the nations, with David as His regent. National distinctions will continue, with the seat of government in Jerusalem. All nations of the earth will be subservient to Israel, since the regathered tribes of Israel will be the center of all things.

The relation of the church to the millennium is not always clear in dispensationalism. Some say that the church will return at the beginning of the millennium and pass through

76. Ohman, *op. cit.*, pp. 28-29.
77. Pentecost, *op. cit.*, p. 56.

it to eternal life. Gaebelein states, "They will enter the kingdom and inherit the same . . . . That they will occupy with
saved Israel a special position in the kingdom, we fully believe . . . ."[78] Others assert that the church will not return
to the earth at all but will be a part of the holy city hovering
above the earth. J. Dwight Pentecost holds this view, asserting
that at the second advent of Christ the church will be transferred from heaven to the city in "the air over the earth,"
where it is joined by the then resurrected Old Testament saints,
and that this constitutes the eternal state. "From that heavenly
city she will reign with him."[79]

The significant thing, however, is not the relation of the
church to Israel during this period, but the relation to the
cross. It is difficult to understand dispensationalism at this
point. Many assert that the grace of the resurrected Christ will
be applicable, but this is not consistent with the doctrine
that the gospel of the kingdom is different from the gospel
of grace.

The temple is to be rebuilt and the sacrifices re-instituted.
The relation of this sacrifical system to the death of Christ is
"commemorative," not anticipatory. By temple ritual and a
system of sacrifice Israel is to commemorate the wonders of
the death of Christ, even as she unknowingly did by way of
anticipation in the Old Testament. However, the question may
well be asked: How can a temple sacrifice commemorate the
death of Christ, when entrance into the kingdom will have
been on the basis of the gospel of the kingdom, not the gospel
of grace? For any act to commemorate the death of Christ it
would have to be based on the death of Christ. This becomes
even more difficult to understand in a system which asserts
that had Israel accepted the original offer to the kingdom
during the earthly life of Christ, it would have been established then. Would the cross have been necessary? Of what,
then, would the continued sacrifices of Judaism have been commemorative?

The historic faith has viewed the millennium as a time when
the *church* would reign with Christ, and though Israel was
to have a special place in that reign, it was to be established

78. Gaebelein, *The Gospel of Matthew*, II, 248.
79. J. Dwight Pentecost, *Things to Come*. Findlay, Ohio: Dunham Publishing Co., 1958, pp. 577-578.

on the basis of grace arising out of Christ's sacrificial death. The blessed hope of the church has been Christ's returning for the *church,* to establish His reign through the *church,* so that every tongue should confess His pre-eminence in the *church.* The blessed hope for the dispensationalists, seemingly, is that Christ will rapture the parenthetical church so that He may reign through *Israel,* not the church.

All of this is, of course, a matter of debate. The interpretation of details is so varied that not even dispensationalists reach full agreement. The principle involved, however, is important. Which is the object of God's blessing, the church for whom Christ died, or the Israel of the Abrahamic covenant? Historic premillennialism has unquestionably stressed the church, making Israel's role conditional upon the same grace given to the church. Dispensational hermeneutics, by making such a sharp distinction between the two, separates itself from that heritage.

The Eternal State

Consistent with their rigid literalism, responsible dispensationalists teach that the "new Jerusalem" of Revelation 21 and 22 is an actual city where the church will dwell eternally. The city will not be in heaven, but will have a physical location. The saints of the church, who have been with God in heaven, will now be transferred to this new city for the rest of eternity. It follows, naturally, that it must also be the abode of God.

> Immediately we see the new heaven and new earth and the New Jerusalem descending to the New earth (21:1, 2), we are told, "Behold, the tabernacle of God is with men" — the former heaven and earth having disappeared. The object of the new heaven and earth is to bring about this — *that God shall eternally have His home* in this capitol city of the new creation! . . . . No other eternal habitation of God is seen than this of the New Creation's capitol! Always before, God was in heaven and man upon earth. Now this city has come down, created by God for His dwelling, we cannot conceive of His *real* presence and worship being elsewhere.[80]

J. Dwight Pentecost maintains this same idea when he writes, "This city is not only the dwelling place of God, Father, Son,

80. William R. Newell, *The Book of Revelation.* Chicago: Grace Publications, 1941 p. 353. (Italics in original.)

and Holy Spirit, but is the dwelling place of the bride, the Lamb's wife (Rev. 21:9) as well."[81] He adds further, "From this consideration, then, it may be stated that the city is to be inhabited by God, by the Church, and by the redeemed of Israel, and by the redeemed of all ages, together with the unfallen angels."[82] Walvoord attributes an extreme literalness to it:

> A most outstanding feature is the dimension of the city which is given as 1500 miles square and also 1500 high. Such a dimension quite unfamiliar even to a modern world with its high buildings would provide a city of impressive and spacious dimensions as the seat of God's eternal government and dwelling place for the saints. Expositors differ as to whether the city is in the form of a cube or a pyramid though the latter seems more likely. If in the form of a pyramid, it is possible that the throne of God will be at the top and the river of life will wend its way from the throne down the various levels of the city. In these brief terms is given a description of the ultimate resting place of the saints beyond which Scripture revelation does not go in its unfolding of the endless ages of eternity.[83]

Historic premillennialism has not interpreted this verse so literally. Though there is naturally some variance, the general interpretation has been that either it applies in some way to the millennium, or is symbolic, not literal, of the future age.

The Apostate Nature of Christendom

One of the earliest principles to emerge in Darby's thought was the distinction between the true church and Christendom. The true church contains only those who have been saved, a limited number out of the mass of professing Christians. Ecclesiastical organization has corrupted the organized church — the eternal, visible church that is seen here on earth. The church, therefore, cannot be described in terms of the organized structure which is seen today, but only in terms of the relation of the believer to Christ. The church is heavenly, not earthly: the individual believer is not baptized into a church here on earth, but into a heavenly relation with Christ.[84]

In practical consequences, this caused Darby to distrust all

81. Pentecost, *op. cit.*, p. 575.
82. *Ibid.*, p. 576.
83. John F. Walvoord, "The Doctrine of the Millennium," *Bibliotheca Sacra*, 115:4:301 (Oct.-Dec. 1958).
84. Darby's doctrine of the church is developed more fully in Chapter IV.

organized ecclesiastical systems (though he created one himself). Two ideas, the individual *heavenly* relation to Christ as constituting the church, and the distrust of ecclesiastical systems, combined to establish a spirit of separatism in Darby's movement. All who did not agree with Darby's interpretation were characterized as "not having the truth" or as "not understanding the divine plan of the ages," and therefore as somewhat "apostate."

Has not this spirit characterized dispensationalism in its development? Is it more than a coincidence that dispensationalism has been associated prominently with the theology of interdenominational and independent churches? Why has it been resisted so steadily by denominations which are rooted in the theology of the Reformation? Why has the issue of dispensational truth divided denominations and caused ecclesiastical rupture? We do not pretend to answer these questions, but only to raise the problem of how dispensationalism might have affected the spirit of separatism which characterizes some parts of evangelicalism today.

With some features of the foregoing exposition, certain dispensationalists will no doubt disagree. The purpose of this chapter has not been, however, to explore all the details of this view, but rather to survey the main outlines of dispensationalism as contrasted with historic premillennialism. Nor has the foregoing been an attempt to refute dispensationalism: the purpose has been simply to show its logical structure as a whole.

It may well be, as some dispensationalists argue, that even if their system has no historical continuity with the faith of the church, it is still a proper interpretation of the Scriptures. We do not argue that point at all. We seek only to establish what it is, to reveal the source from whence it has come, and to point out its implications for contemporary church life. We leave its evaluation to the reader.

We turn now to a study of the origin of dispensationalism. What kind of a man was J. N. Darby? What were the circumstances in which his theology was fashioned? What is his doctrine of the church? What were the practical consequences of his theology of the church for his own day? What is its implication for our day? We shall have to answer these questions if we are to evaluate dispensationalism properly.

CHAPTER II

J. N. DARBY: AN ESTIMATE OF THE MAN

MANY PEOPLE find a system exceedingly fascinating which repudiates all ecclesiastical pretension and proposes to submerge all sectarian distinctions in a simple gathering of believers to Christ. Its attractiveness is greatly enhanced if it professes marked biblical simplicity together with an equally marked aversion to theological systems, and if its disciples are distinguished by humility, sanctity, and zeal. If, moreover, it presumes to supply the latest results of a thoroughly spiritual insight into Scripture, in an age ready to welcome any means of establishing a recovering harmony between the spirit of the Reformation and the genius of modern free inquiry, it will be sure to command a wide audience.[1]

In the early nineteenth century the Brethren movement, known popularly as "Plymouth Brethrenism," made such an appeal to large numbers, not only in the environs of its origin — Ireland and England — but throughout Europe, the North American continent, and Australia.

Credit for the impetus of this movement is due largely to the efforts of John Nelson Darby, who, though not the founder, became the prime mover in co-ordinating and propagating its doctrines. No examination of the total movement can disregard the influences of this man, nor can influences be adequately evaluated without a study of its history and character.

The known facts about Darby's birth and early life establish his ancestry as "a highly honorable family,"[2] his uncle being

1. G. T. Stokes, *Plymouth Brethrenism: Its Ecclesiastical and Doctrinal Teachings; with a Sketch of Its History.* London: Hodder & Stoughton, 1874, Third thousand, p. 3. Reprinted from *British Quarterly*, Oct., 1873.
2. W. Blair Neatby, *A History of the Plymouth Brethren.* London: Hodder & Stoughton, 1901, p. 17.

Admiral Darby of Nile celebrity.[3] Born of Irish parents in London, November, 1800, his early years were spent in Ireland, where he attended Westminster School. At the age of fifteen he entered Trinity College, Dublin, as a fellow-commoner, and graduated as a Classical Gold Medalist in the summer of 1819 when little more than eighteen years of age.[4]

After gaduation he entered the legal profession and was called to the Irish Chancery Bar in 1822, being associated with his brother-in-law, who later became the Lord Chief Justice of Ireland. All records extant indicate his natural abilities to have been such as to assure him a brilliant career in this profession. His subsequent conversion, however, caused him to abandon the profession after one year, and in 1825 he was ordained a deacon in the Church of England by Archbishop Magee of Dublin, and was appointed to the curacy of a large and struggling parish, Enniskerry,[5] in County Wicklow.[6]

The success of his labors there can be measured by the testimony of those acquainted with his ministry. He threw himself into his work with a compassion and abandonment of self, which he later exhibited in the Brethren movement, as is evident from the testimony of Prof. Francis W. Newman:

> He took orders and became an indefatigable curate in the mountains of Wicklow. Every evening he sallied forth to teach in the cabins, and roving far and wide over mountains and amid bogs, was seldom home before midnight. By such exertion, his strength was undermined; he suffered in his limbs that not lameness only, but yet more serious results were feared. He did not fast on purpose . . . but his long walks through wild country and amongst indigent people inflicted on him such a severe privation; moreover, as he ate whatever food offered itself, food unpalateable and often indigestible to him, his whole frame might have vied in emaciation with a monk of La Trappe . . . . The stamp of heaven seemed . . . clear, in a frame so wasted by austerity, so superior to worldly pomp, and so partaking of all their indigencies. That a dozen such men would have done more to convert all Ireland to Protestantism, than the

3. Thomas Croskery, "John Nelson Darby," *The Catholic Presbyterian*. London: James Nisbet & Co., VII (June, 1882) , 441.

4. Hy Pickering, *Chief Men Among the Brethren*. London: Pickering & Inglis, 1913, p. 12.

5. W. G. Turner, *John Nelson Darby, A Biography*. London: C. A. Hammond, 1926, p. 28.

6. Henry Groves, *Memoirs of Lord Congleton*. London: John F. Shaw & Co., 1884, p. 13.

whole appartus of the Church Establishment, was ere long my conviction. . . .7

A tremendous spiritual awakening attended his efforts, especially among the Roman Catholics with whom he worked. By his own statement Catholics were "becoming Protestants at the rate of 600 to 800 a week."8 Such remarkable results indicate the fervent passion and sincerity with which Darby labored. This is all the more remarkable for being achieved in the duration of one year's ministry, since the following year he appeared before Archbishop Magee to be formally ordained as a minister.

While he was in Dublin for ordination, the Archbishop issued a decree which was subsequently to change the life of Darby, and to lead him from the Church of England.

> The archbishop delivered a charge, and the clergy published a declaration addressed to Parliament denouncing the Roman Catholic Church, and claiming special favor and protection for themselves on avowed Erastian principles. They based their demands simply on the ground that Romanism was opposed to the State, while their own system was allied with, if not subservient to, it.9

Darby's mind so revolted against such a low conception of the church that he privately circulated a tract denouncing the move as unscriptural, but the petition was of no avail. He returned to his curacy bitterly disillusioned, for the demand that all converts to the church must swear allegiance to the king was inherent in the decree. This was unthinkable to Darby's mind, since it not only seemed to be a mere transference of allegiance from the Pope to the King, but prevented the convert from fully realizing his responsibility of obedience to Christ.

After the decree his outstanding success with Catholics ceased almost immediately. He retired to a prayerful study of the

7. Francis W. Newman, *Phases of Faith, or, Passages from the History of My Creed.* London: John Chapman, 1850, p. 28. While Newman refers to the person he describes as "The Irish Clergyman," and never calls him by name, it is clear from association of fact that he refers to Darby.

8. J. N. Darby, as quoted by Neatby, *op. cit.,* p. 16; J. N. Darby, *Disendowment — Disestablishment: A Word to the Protestants of Ireland, in a Letter to the Venerable Archdeacon Stopford,* Col. Writ., Eccl. Vol. IV, p. 437, where he undoubtedly refers to this as "many hundreds in the week."

9. G. T. Stokes, "J. N. Darby," *Contemporary Review.* London: Isbister & Co., October, 1885, 48:538 (1885).

position of the church in world affairs, and in 1829 published a pamphlet entitled *Considerations on the Nature and Unity of the Church of Christ,* which has been called "the Brethren's first pamphlet."[10]

In the interval between 1826, when the decree was first issued, and 1828, when he published his first tract, Darby passed through a period of deep study and earnest reflection. Qualms and increasingly serious doubts which had perturbed him before now clamored for a decision. He would not disobey the diocesan rule, but he believed it to be a dishonor to the Christian ministry.

After the failure of his protest against the decree, and consistent with his changing concepts, he looked for some body which might satisfy his aspirations for a spiritual communion on scriptural principles, not just political expediency, and soon found it in a group of men who met together for mutual edification through prayer and Bible study. During the winter of 1827-28 he met regularly with these friends,[11] and it was this group, which, under his leadership, was destined to become the Brethren movement.[12]

An Estimate of the Man

Any estimate of Darby — as a man, author-scholar, and religious leader — must inevitably involve contradictions and contrasts, since many of his personality traits were diametrically opposed to each other. Simple in taste, benevolent in disposition, kind in temperament, considerate in his awareness of others, humble in spirit, sympathetic in nature, he was at the same time ruthless in controversy, belligerent to those who opposed him, jealous of his position of authority, and exacting in his demands. Every attempt to evaluate him must always

10. Neatby, *op. cit.,* p. 18, on which he comments, "It was the expression of a tendency which, though rapidly coming to a head, was yet only a tendency . . . . The tract contains some forcible passages and attacks the existing order with a good deal of power; but it is strikingly lacking in definiteness of suggestion, and is plainly either the writing of a man who does not see his way clearly, or who deliberately prefers to keep his own counsel."

11. This is not to suggest that Darby had broken with the Church of England at this time. The cause of the break and the subsequent rise of the Brethren group are discussed in the next chapter.

12. Stokes, *op. cit.,* p. 538.

hold these two aspects of his character in contradistinction. At the same time, no estimate of the man will be honest if it does not attempt to find a ground of agreement between them.

The single motivation of Darby's entire life was his love for Christ. If any principle is sufficient to explain the multiple facets of his personality, most probably it is this love. Because of it he has been called "a saint of the highest and purest stamp."[13] At the same time, this love for Christ caused him to strike relentlessly against any, even close friends, whom he thought to be subverting the truth of Christ's gospel.

In an age of rampant materialism, the simplicity and frugality of his life rivaled that of the early saints. After renouncing a promising career in law, he sacrificed the delights of marriage and children in order to pursue his chosen work without distraction. He had little concern for his own person, as is shown by the following description:

> His bodily presence was indeed "weak." A fallen cheek, a blood-shot eye, crippled limb resting on crutch, a seldom shaved beard, a shabby suit of clothes, and a generally neglected person, drew at first pity, with wonder to see such a figure in a drawing room . . . . With keen logical powers, he had warm sympathy, solid judgment of character, thoughtful tenderness, and total self-abandonment.[14]

He preferred being with the poor, for he was essentially humble in spirit. This characteristic endeared him to the folk of humble status, and was perhaps one of the secrets of his success with the poor Romanists of Ireland and the peasants of France and Switzerland.

> In middle life he trudged on foot through a large part of France and Switzerland, sometimes refreshing himself on the way with acorns, at other times thankful to have an egg for his dinner . . . .

> In his own house, all was simplicity and self-denial.
> Thoughtful for others, he was indifferent as to comforts for himself . . . . his clothes were plain, and he wore them to shabbiness, though punctiliously clean in his person. In Limerick once, kind friends

---

13. Editor of *Southern Review*, as quoted by W. G. Turner, *John Nelson Darby*, London: C. A. Hammond, 1951, p. 67. The reader will note that this volume is different from *John Nelson Darby, a Biography* (1926) by the same author and publisher. While the two books contain much material which is identical even to the phrasing, the later volume provides much added material.

14. Newman, *op. cit.*, p. 27.

took advantage of his sleep to replace the old with new, which he put on without a word.[15]

It is not surprising that such self-abandonment should result in a life of humble service. Trained as a scholar among the intellectuals, he found peace in laboring among the poor and ignorant. His unchallenged consistency, sincerity, and unwearied service to the faith commanded the reverence and admiration of those who recognized in him a spiritual guide.[16]

Incidents illustrating his singularly benevolent nature are numerous. While addressing a meeting he would roll up his coat as a pillow for a sleeping child whose uncomfortable attitude he had noticed. On one of his numerous voyages he paced the deck all night with a restless child in his arms so that the tired mother could get some rest. Though possessing little wealth he was known to assist immigrants in their passage, provide clothing for underprivileged children, or assume responsibility for purchase for medicine for certain destitute families. On occasion he labored at the menial task of some of his friends who were ill, to prevent them from losing their employment. While visiting in various cities in Britain, the Continent, and America, he preferred to stay with the poor instead of the rich. One incident is recorded of his arrival in a certain Swiss city where the elite of the assembly were adroitly maneuvering for the privilege of entertaining the "great man." Appraising the situation at a glance, he inquired as to who usually entertained the visiting brothers. When all eyes turned to a poor meek man standing in the rear, he replied, "I will stay where the other brethren stay."[17]

> His kindly thoughtfulness for his poorer brethren, both in temporal and spiritual needs, was most marked.
> His patience with honest ignorance, his ready tact, his manliness of character, and hearty sympathy endeared him to many, especially among the poorer classes.[18]

Nor was this place of supremacy confined to his relation with the poor, for he was held in high regard by men of scholarly attainment. On a visit to Oxford University he "instantaneously assumed the place of universal father-confessor, as

---

15. William Kelly, as quoted by Turner, *John Nelson Darby*, p. 77.
16. Turner, *John Nelson Darby, A Biography*, p. 62.
17. Turner, *John Nelson Darby*, p. 35 *et. passim*.
18. *Ibid.*, pp. 34-35.

if he had been a known and long-trusted friend. His insight
into character, and tenderness pervading his austerity, so
opened young men's hearts that day after day there was no
end of secret closeting with him."[19]

> In spite of the strong revulsion which I felt against some of the
> peculiarities of this remarkable man, I for the first time in my life
> found myself under the dominion of a superior. When I remember,
> how even those bowed down before him, who had been to him in
> the place of parents — accomplished and experienced minds, — I
> cease to wonder in the retrospect, that he riveted me in such bond-
> age . . . . In his reply I always expected to find a higher portion
> of God's Spirit, than in any I could frame for myself. In order
> to learn divine truth, it became a surer process to consult him than
> to search for myself. . . .[20]

Darby as a Religious Leader

The motivating power of Darby's love for Christ is most
clearly demonstrated in his activity as a religious leader. If
any man ever dominated a religious movement by personal
magnetism, it was Darby. His control over his followers had
been termed "nothing short of popery."[21]

> As the leader of a religious party, he wields more power than all
> the bishops of England put together. He has attained, indeed, an in-
> fluence and authority among the Brethren not to be found in any
> other Protestant community on earth.[22]

While it cannot be denied that much of his immense influence over his followers was the result of his own ambition,
a careful analysis of his life and work will reveal that again
and again he took a definite stand on certain issues "for the
cause of Christ." He professed to require a New Testament
precedent for every act or doctrine, and never ceased to apply
the Scriptures to himself.

> . . . I admired his unflinching consistency. For now, as always,
> all he said was based on texts aptly quoted and logically enforced.
> He made me more and more ashamed of Political Economy and
> Moral Philosophy and all Sciences; all of which ought to be "counted
> dross for the excellency of the knowledge of Christ Jesus our Lord."

19. Newman, *op. cit.*, p. 45.
20. *Ibid.*, p. 33.
21. Neatby, *op. cit.*, p. 192.
22. Stokes, *op. cit.*, p. 12.

For the first time in my life I saw a man earnestly turning into reality the principles which others professed with their lips only.[23]

Darby's leadership was neither the product of a morbid spirituality nor of mere religious emotionalism, but the result of a clear apprehension of the object for which he had been apprehended by Christ. He was ever mindful of the spiritual needs of his followers, and his thoughts, both in speech and writing, constantly soared to the spiritual solutions for all things. Though he was active in religous controversy, his mind was constantly upon Christ and the truth of His church. In the preface to one of his controversial tracts he writes,

> It is far more happy to be occupied in considering the riches of the grace of God, and of the love of Christ than to be discussing questions of office and institutions. It is however at times necessary to speak about these also, when they are put forward with a view of troubling the peace of Christians and of exciting their minds . . . . It is, then, in order to clear up these contested points and to tranquillize the minds of Christians that I would say a few words upon office and gifts. I do so, however, with the most fervent desire that each one, after having been enlightened on the subject, may turn from these questions and leave them entirely alone, so as to be occupied with Christ, and His exhaustless love and immeasurable grace. For it is that which nourishes and edifies, while questions tend to dryness and barrenness of soul.[24]

Darby's spirit in controversy reveals again the many facets of his character. When he thought the cause of Christ was being jeopardized he became ruthless, letting no one stand in his way. Close friends of many years' acquaintance were called "seducers of the faith," while appellations such as "enemies of Christ," "perverters of the saints," "our adversaries" were used to denounce those with whom he disputed.

Some of his most bitter denunciations, it must be admitted, were based on apparent jealousy for his own position of authority.

> For the first time I perceived that so vehement a champion of the sufficiency of the Scriptures, so staunch an opposer of creed and churches, was wedded to an extra-scriptural creed of his own, by which he tested the spiritual state of his brethren.[25]

23. Newman, *op. cit.*, p. 29.
24. J. N. Darby, *On Gifts and Offices in the Church.* Col. Writ., Eccl. Vol. III, p. 1.
25. Newman, *op. cit.*, p. 58.

It is this aspect of Darby's personality that does him no credit. In fact, it almost destroyed the pure ground of fellowship upon which Brethrenism was based. He cannot be commended for relentlessly prolonging his controversies, for imposing overly harsh demands for agreement, or for forcing such a narrow limit of fellowship upon all of Brethrenism. These derogatory aspects of his character must be frankly admitted. They cannot, however, wholly detract from a great heart filled with love for Christ and passionately determined to do all that was necessary to protect His cause.

While Darby was vicious in controversy, he professed a natural hesitancy to enter such conflicts. As a preface to many of his controversial tracts he acknowledges this hesitance.[26] In one he states,

> My intention is not controversy . . . . It may be perhaps said to me: — If desirous of avoiding controversy, why do you enter upon such subjects? I reply that, along with a sincere desire for peace, it is not right on that account to refrain from setting forth important principles . . . . Although the brother who has replied to me blames me, I continue to respect and love him . . . . I hope not to be found wanting in love whilst making a few remarks on my brother's work . . . .[27]

Because of the youth of the author, he delayed for eleven months in answering a pamphlet entitled, "Ministry As Opposed to Hierarchism and Chiefly Religious Radicalism," in which the author attacked "Plymouthism," "not wanting to condemn what was youthful enthusiasm in an unfair and undue manner." However, when the pamphlet was approved by the Lay Society and by the Report of the Evangelical Society of Geneva, he retorted in severe criticism with such expressions as "a temerity which erases with the dash of a pen all that has been written on the subject from the time of Chrysostom . . . self-contradiction of the grossest kind . . . a contempt for the Word . . . deliberate misrepresentation of the Scripture."[28]

26. As in Eccl. Vol. I, pp. 169, 240, 314, 405, 415, 420; Eccl. Vol. III, pp. 266, 305, 369; Doc. Vol. VII, p. 228, etc.

27. J. N. Darby, *Some Further Developments of the Principles Set Forth in the Pamphlet, entitled, "On the Formation of Churches," and Reply to Some Objections Made to these Principles,* Col. Writ., Eccl. Vol. I, pp. 238-40.

28. J. N. Darby, *On the Presence and Action of the Holy Ghost in the Church,* Col. Writ., Doc. Vol. I, p. 318.

Other evidences of Darby's hesitancy to enter controversy are reflected in his attitude toward his purpose in writing.

> The writer has only to repeat his entire regret at the occasion of it [writing the tract]. He has refrained from any statement of, or invective against, the flagrant and painful abuses, which must and ought to shock the conscience, connected with the subject; or attributing motives to those implicated in what the tract charges as evil . . . .[29]

In the preface of one of his most controversial tracts he states, "They were written for edification, not controversy."[30]

In spite of his hesitancy for controversy, he viewed it as an integral part of his task. He felt it his duty to refute everything which might subvert the growth of the weak in the faith. He had no interest in a purely intellectual debate, but desired to expose the basic fallacies of his opponents so that their errors might be plain to all.

> If I have to take my adversaries up, because they still carry on their warfare, and Satan is using them for mischief, I here declare I will not spare them, nor fail, with God's help, to make plain the tenets and doctrines which are at the bottom of all this.[31]

It is strange that a man of such deep spirituality should at times exhibit a haughty, imperious, peremptory, and intractable nature. Every biographer of Darby is constantly faced with these contradictory traits of his personality, and few have treated them in their proper perspective. Those who are not in accord with his general views usually stress his controversial nature and picture him as an arrogant, pompous *imperium*. His followers tend to regard all his adverse qualities as arising from his zeal, and consequently excuse him. He was neither perfectly good nor utterly bad, though he often displayed the characteristics of both. His deep spirituality, love for Christ, and kindly regard for others cannot be erased by his tyrannical qualities, nor, on the other hand, can this antagonistic nature be ignored.

The most logical explanation is that he was a man filled with a passion: a passion that erupted in a tumultuous crusade

29. J. N. Darby, *Reply to the Two Leading Articles of the Christian Journal entitled "Our Separating Brethren."* Col. Writ., Eccl. Vol. III, p. 176.

30. J. N. Darby, *The Suffering of Christ*, Col. Writ., Doc. Vol. II, p. 215.

31. *Ibid.*, p 214.

for what he believed to be right. He expressed the secret of his whole life and work as, "Our duty as believers is to be witnesses of what we believe."[32] He carried this out in a life of indefatigable activity. If this purpose interrupted his fraternal relations, he did not hesitate to sacrifice them on the altar of duty, counting it a solemn responsibility to consider the cause of Christ as paramount. He did not doubt that the sole reason of his existence was to serve: executing this conviction drove him to bitter extremes in his relationship with others. Consequently most of his life, and a large portion of his writings, were spent in controversy. Perhaps his zeal for maintaining doctrinal purity usurped control of his personality until his antagonistic spirit became a part of that personality. F. W. Newman seems to suggest this.

> . . . this gentleman has every where displayed a wonderful power of bending other minds to his own, and even stamping upon them the tones of his voice and all sorts of slavish imitation. Over the general results of his action I have long deeply mourned, as blunting his natural tenderness and sacrificing his wisdom to the Letter, dwarfing men's understandings, contracting their hearts, crushing their moral sensibilities, and setting those at variance who ought to love: *yet oh! how specious it was in the beginning! he only wanted men "to submit their understanding to God," that is to the Bible, that is, to his interpretation.*[33]

Darby as an Author

Darby began writing for the public at the age of twenty-eight, and from then until his death at the advanced age of eighty-two, there followed in quick succession treatises covering the widest fields of religious inquiry. His published works number over forty volumes of six hundred pages each, covering ecclesiastical, doctrinal, prophetical, critical, evangelistic, apologetic, practical, expository, and devotional subjects, as well as several volumes of poetry and hymns. Resplendent with his knowledge and use of the Scriptures, they are filled with repeated use of phrases such as "according to the Word of God," "as found in the Word," and "from the Holy Writ." With simple faith in the Scriptures as the inspired Word from whence came all guidance and instruction, he had a single ap-

---

32. J. N. Darby, *Considerations on the Nature and Unity of the Church of Christ*, Col. Writ., Eccl. Vol. I, p. 42.

33. Newman, *op. cit.*, p. 33, (Italics not in original.)

proach: abstaining from the abstract philosophical argument, he simply opened the Bible and absorbed its message with little regard for extraneous study.

. . While pressing the authority of every letter of the Scripture with an unshrinking vehemence that I never saw surpassed, yet, with a common inconsistency, [he] showed more indifference towards learned historical and critical evidence on the side of Christianity; and indeed, unmercifully exposed erudition to scorn, both by caustic reasoning, and by irrefragable quotation of texts.34

One of his chief contributions to the theological literature of Brethrenism is his *Translation of the Holy Scripture,* "an entirely free and independent rendering of the whole original text, using all known helps."35

The Revisers used his New Testament, and were astonished at the amount of painstaking research exceeding that of most, if not all, as two of the best in the company wrote to the late William Kelly . . . . *In the translation of the Scriptures the literary was made to give place to the literal,* and hence it is characterized by a certain abruptness of style. This, however, is more than compensated for (sic) by the invaluable notes with which it is furnished, and which in the judgment of competent critics betokens true scientific scholarship.36

34. *Ibid.,* p. 42. This does not mean that Darby did not have the critical apparatus at his command, for he was well schooled in all techniques of scholarship.

35. Turner, *John Nelson Darby,* p. 53.

36. *Ibid.* Turner, undoubtedly a Plymouth Brother himself, and an ardent follower of Darbyism, is understandably profuse in his praise of Darby's translation. Not all writers would agree, however, as is attested by two reviews to which the reader is directed. *Darbyism and Its New Bible, Taken from an Article Communicated to "The Sword and Trowel," Monthly Magazine of Rev. C. H. Spurgeon,* London: W. Macintosh, 1874, p. 18, comments, "We don't even mention the other renderings in his new Bible, just as serious and erroneous as the above; must less notice the transposition of tenses and prepositions, or the awkward English diction throughout. Suffice it to say, that some renderings are good, and some of the notes are good; but, taken as a whole, with a great display of learning, the ignorance of the results of modern criticism is almost incredible. And the fatal upsetting of vital doctrines condemns the work altogether as more calculated to promote scepticism than true religion — the most sacred subjects being handled with irreverent familiarity." *Mr. Darby's New Bible and It's Announcement by One Who Writes on Behalf of Many,* London: W. Mackintosh, 1868, p. 14, evaluates it as, "Endless blunders, errors, mistranslations, confounding of moods, tenses and preposition — do not surprise us."

Such criticism is extremely harsh, and it is certain that the author

While he wrote indefatigably, he was indifferent to literary distinction. He was primarily concerned with the glory of Christ, not self-aggrandizement. He valued simplicity of thought and understanding above style; consequently, many of his sentences are complex and involved, with paragraph contained within paragraph, in an attempt to explain and guard against misunderstanding. Unfortunately, his attempts at clarity only confuse the reader, since his style becomes so abstruse that the reader loses the original thought in the complexity of qualifying phrases.

An example of his involved style illustrates the plight of the reader:

> They have seen, on a subsequent evening (where, as I undoubtedly judge Satan made a seemingly overpowering effort to upset all they were doing, and hinder, by distracting and speaking them down, their acting on what they had been led to), that the same brethren, after listening to all those who came thus to interpret them from other places (proving they rejected none), could adhere, as led and guided of God, with firmness to that which they had been led to by Him; and could prove, when thus put to the severest test, with little or nothing really to help them from without, that God's blessed presence in their weakness could give patience and grace, and deference to the weakest within, and resist the noisiest and most clamorous from without; nor was there the slightest idea of rejecting the help and assistance, and spiritual wisdom of those whose experience and faithfulness they trusted in, but the glad acceptance of it; as such as have more or less that character acted just in setting the matters before their conscience.[37]

This abstruseness of style is not due to lack of scholarship on Darby's part. He was well versed in Greek, Latin, Hebrew, French, and German. His writings reveal an extensive knowledge of philosophy, history (particularly ecclesiastical), and the sciences. He has been called the Tertullian of the nine-

---

is at passionately prejudiced against Darby as Turner is for him. Without doubt, however, there is a close parallel between Darby's translation and his doctrine. It would be difficult to determine whether the translation influenced the doctrine, or the doctrine influenced the translation, since the chronology is not always clear, but it is certainly evident that his involved translation is consistent with his involved doctrinal structure.

37. J. N. Darby, *Account of Proceedings at Rawstone Street*, Col. Writ., Eccl. Vol. IV, pp. 225-26.

teenth century,[38] and the Goliath of Dissent.[39] His style was certainly not due to lack of discipline as a student, since he devoted his whole life to studious activities. ". . . he was habitually a hard worker, from early morn devoted to his own reading the Word and prayer . . . . Indeed, whole days were frequently devoted to Scripture reading wherever he moved, at home or abroad."[40]

Two factors may be said to have contributed to his style: his overwhelming passion to state and defend the truth of the gospel, and a hurried disregard for form. Many of his tracts are evidently nothing more than sermon notes, possibly jotted down in a hurry. Others seem to be hardly more than mere first drafts; some even to be uncorrected notes of lectures or sermons taken down by others.

> Mr. Darby was deliberate and prayerful in weighing a scripture; but he wrote rapidly; as thoughts arose in his spirit, and often with scarcely a word changed. He delighted in concatenated sentences, sometimes with a parenthesis within a parenthesis, to express the truth fully, and with guards against misconception. An early riser and indefatigable worker, he yet had not the time to express himself as briefly and clearly as he could wish. "You write to be read and understood," he once said playfully to me: "I only think on paper." This made his writings, to the uninitiated, anything but pleasant reading, and to a hasty glance almost unintelligible; so that many, even among the highly educated believers, turned away, because of their inability to penetrate sentences so involved.[41]

He was doubtless conscious of this difficulty, since he felt it necessary in the preface of one of his tracts to state,

> It [what he had written] seems to me that as it stands it is quite sufficiently clear to any upright mind. I am not so foolish as to think that all the expressions in it are the best, or absolutely exact or just, as if I was (sic) inspired. . . . To the humblest and weakest of God's saints, I should gladly explain my meaning . . . .[42]

Although his style was poor, the force of his written work cannot be denied. One opponent, after an exchange of tracts

38. Pickering, *op. cit.*, p. 11.
39. D'Arcy Sirr, *Memoirs of Archbishop Le Poer Trench*, p. 344, as quoted by Neatby, *op. cit.*, p. 49.
40. William Kelly, as quoted by Turner, *John Nelson Darby*, p. 77.
41. William Kelly, as quoted by Turner, *op. cit.*, pp. 72-73.
42. Darby, *Sufferings of Christ*, p. 214.

with him, remarked, "J.N.D. writes with a pen in one hand
and a thunderbolt in the other."[43]

> . . . his style is execrable; his grammar bad; yet the criticism is
> just that "Those obscure, uncouth, ungrammatical, torturous sen-
> tences, which only excite our contempt, enter into the very bone
> of the victims, and paralyzes them in the inner man." So far as
> we may judge by his writings, he seems to be a man of iron will,
> without bowel or sympathies . . . . He certainly brings into theo-
> logical literature and controversy a plainness of speech that has
> almost gone out of fashion in the churches . . . .[44]

Most of Darby's writings are polemic. Many are replies to
tracts by others, in which he either answers a charge or seizes
upon some statement from the opponent with which to construct his own view. In most of these the reader is subjected
to an endless series of references to the tract in question,
the context of which he knows nothing — a circumstance which
he finds most disconcerting.

Neatby gives us a judicious over-all appraisal of Darby as
an author:

> He carried his neglect of appearances into his written and spoken
> composition; and that to such an extent that the style of his writing
> to the reader of today seems half ludicrous, half disgusting . . . . [but]
> all misgivings as to the teacher's sincerity — even as to his absorbing
> earnestness of aim — disappears before it. Darby's own account of
> the matter was that he could have equalled the rhetorical flights of
> the great masters, but he never thought it worthwhile . . . . it is
> hard to read Darby's better works without fancying that a noble
> eloquence was really at his command, if only he had chosen to
> cultivate it. Bad as his style is, it is the badness of an almost
> incredible carelessness rather than a defective power.[45]

Conclusion

Darby the man is difficult to estimate fairly. All who knew
him in the early years of his ministry portray him as filled
with saintly virtue, while unprejudiced testimony about his
later years reveals a nature warped, caustic, and even at times
vicious. Though he always maintained that his motives were
pure, personal ambition and selfishness were often undeniably
reflected in his actions.

43. Turner, *op. cit.*, p. 31.
44. Stokes, *op. cit.*, p. 12.
45. Neatby, *op. cit.*, pp. 49-50.

It would be altogether too simple to attribute all his later actions to a personality that had become warped by personal ambition, and conclude that this was the man, John Darby. Even while he was involved in these later controversies, he wrote some tracts that show deep spiritual insights. Suffice it to say that he stamped his movement with his own personality. Much of its spiritual atmosphere undoubtedly belongs to his influence; and certainly its interpretative principles, its divisive compartmentalization of the redemptive plan of God, its literalness as to prophetic interpretation, and its separatist spirit may be traced to this personality. Perhaps it is too broad a summary to say that Darby's personality influenced directly the spirit of contemporary dispensationalism, but certainly the pattern which he set into motion is reflected in it.

Chapter III

HISTORICAL BACKGROUNDS TO DISPENSATIONALISM[1]

WHATEVER ELSE may be said of the origin of the Plymouth Brethren movement, it cannot be stated that it started at a specific place or time. Attempts to trace its history can only begin with a series of independent groups meeting at various locations. It did not develop, on the one hand, by a slow and laborious process, or, on the other hand, by the sudden genius of one man. We do know, however, that the movement gained impetus through the amalgamation of several of these small meetings, and that after these common meetings its growth was furthered by several early leaders: A. N. Groves, B. W. Newton, W. H. Dorman, E. Cronin, J. G. Bellett, S. P. Tregelles, and J. N. Darby.

The founder of Brethrenism as a system, however, was undeniably J. N. Darby, who became its energizing and guiding spirit throughout. "In the grandeur of his conception, in the irresistible vehemence of his will, in his consummate strategical instinct, in his genius for administration . . . in his immense personal ascendency, he stands unrivalled amongst the Brethren."[2]

Of the main unaffiliated groups in Ireland and England between 1825 and 1832, only Dublin, Plymouth, and Bristol contributed directly to the origin of the movement. From the standpoint of date and influence, it is clear that the Dublin meeting preceded the other two. If the origin of the movement

1. It may be felt by some that the history of the Brethren (Darbyites) through which the author now leads the reader is extraneous to the subject. However, it is the author's opinion that no one can adequately understand either the doctrines or the spirit of dispensationalism unless he understands these backgrounds out of which they have arisen, since the temper of the early days so vitally affected the formation of its hermeneutics and doctrines.

2. W. Blair Neatby, *A History of the Plymouth Brethren.* London: Hodder & Stoughton, 1901, p. 44.

must be localized, Dublin must be regarded as the place from which its spirit emanated — a spirit without which the independent and often divergent meetings could never have combined into a movement.[3]

The history of the Dublin meeting can be seen in its proper perspective only by considering the personalities involved. Most prominent of these early leaders was A. N. Groves. Born in 1795, he was trained as a dentist, and entered practice in Plymouth, from whence he later moved to Exeter where he became exceedingly prosperous. From the age of twenty he had felt the call to the mission field, but due to the opposition of his wife, this had been held in abeyance. In 1825, with full concurrence of his wife, he decided to abandon his profession and qualify as an ordained missionary.

He entered Trinity College, Dublin, the same year, but did not reside in Dublin since he needed only to appear for examinations at the end of term. On such visits he met with a group of Christians who gathered for mutual aid in study and prayer.

These people, according to Groves, were "chiefly members of the Establishment who . . . desired to see more devotedness to Christ and union among all the people of God,"[4] and who met together somewhat regular for this purpose.[5]

3. Hy Pickering, *Chief Men Among the Brethren*, London, Pickering & Inglis, 1931, 2nd. edition, p. 23, refers to an earlier meeting conducted in Demerara by a Leonard Strong, a former Church of England curate. "Years before Anthony Norris Groves and his friends, Leonard Strong read the same Bible and found the same principles. So he gave up his living . . . and met simply for worship among his converts, many hundreds of whom followed him. The first meeting was held in a large shed . . . about 2000 being present." It cannot be doubted that this, and perhaps other similar independent meetings occurred, but from the standpoint of historical continuity there is no connection between this group and the movement, and the origin of Brethrenism *as a system* must be focused on Dublin.

4. Mrs. A. N. Groves, *Memoirs of A. N. Groves*. London: G. Morrish, n.d., p. 15.

5. G. T. Stokes, "J. N. Darby," *Contemporary Review*. London: Isbister & Co., October, 48:539 (1885), regards this merely as a "drawing room meeting for prayer and study of Scripture, which even took the place of lighter amusement in a somewhat extensive circle in the Irish metropolis, and which were then quite the rage with all serious minds." Whether this was true or not, subsequent events were to translate it from the realm of a nondescript meeting to a vigorous campaign for truth as its leaders saw it.

In the spring of 1827, J. G. Bellett, a member of the group, related to another, Miss Bessy Paget,

> Groves has just been telling me, that it appears to him from Scripture that believers, meeting together as disciples of Christ, were free to break bread together as their Lord had admonished them, and that, in so far as the practice of the apostles could be a guide, every Lord's Day should be set apart for thus remembering the Lord's death, and obeying his parting command.[6]

Bellett and his friends in Dublin proceeded immediately to do so.

This memorable suggestion seems to have laid the foundation of Brethrenism. The chief members of the group were Groves, Bellett, Francis Hutchinson, and Edward Cronin.[7] There was no disposition to make a break with the Established Church; indeed, some of the members were clergymen, and all continued to worship at times in their own churches without any idea of a mission to protest against ecclesiastical evil.

Groves' churchmanship was still strongly that of the Established Church, so much so that a request to address a dissenting group brought him "repugnance . . . because I really disapproved on principle and saw that it would stand in the way of my procuring ordination . . . . I had never yet been near a dissenting place of worship."[8] After he had given up the idea of completing his education, considering it nonessential, he applied to the Church Missionary Society to work as a layman. However, when informed that he would not be allowed to dispense the sacraments because he was not ordained, he gave up the idea.

The experience, however, led him to a realization of what was to become one of the "cardinal truths" of Brethrenism: the principle of the liberty of all believers to minister in Christ.

> My mind was in great straits; for I saw not yet my liberty of ministry to be from Christ alone, and felt some ordination to be necessary but hated the thought of being made a sectarian. But, one day the thought was brought to my mind, that ordination of any kind to preach the gospel is no requirement of Scripture. To me it was the removal of a mountain. . . . From that moment, I have myself never had a doubt of my own liberty in Christ to

6. Neatby, *op. cit.*, p. 7.
7. Groves, *op. cit.*, p. 40.
8. *Ibid.*, p. 42.

minister the Word; and in my last visit to Dublin I mentioned my views to dear Mr. Bellett and others.9

Bellett records the incident as follows:

Walking down the street one day with him . . . he said to me, "This I doubt not is the mind of God concerning us — we should come together in all simplicity as disciples, not waiting on any pulpit or ministry, but trusting that the Lord would edify us together by ministering as He pleased and saw good from the midst of us."10

Two principles upon which Brethrenism was founded were thus contributed by Groves: that every Lord's Day should be set aside for "breaking of bread" in remembrance of the Lord's death and obedience to His parting command; and that liberty of ministry is from the call of Christ, not by ordination of man. In 1829 he left for India as a faith missionary and thus virtually separated himself from the movement in England.

The exact date upon which Darby came into contact with the Dublin group cannot be stated with certainty, nor can the extent to which the ideas of Groves had developed at the time of his contact. His first contacts were, no doubt, sporadic ones which occurred on his frequent visits to Dublin from his curacy in Wicklow.11 It is probable that he was introduced to the meeting by Bellett,12 whose first reference to him occurs in a letter dated January 31, 1827.13

The first reference to Darby breaking bread with the group places the date in the winter of 1827-28. It is certain that Darby had not at this time resigned from his charge in the Establishment, since Bellett refers to a meeting of "breaking of bread" at a time when "John Darby was still in the county

9. *Ibid.,* p. 46.
10. Henry Groves, *Memoirs of Lord Congleton.* London: John F. Shaw & Co., 1884, p. 15.
11. Andrew Miller, *The Brethren, Their Origin, Progress and Testimony.* London: Pickering and Inglis, n.d., p. 17.
12. Pickering, *op. cit.,* p. 12.
13. An accident which necessitated treatment and a long period of convalescence in Dublin brought Darby's conflicting doubts into focus. "During my solitude, conflicting thoughts increased; but much exercise of soul had the effect of causing the Scriptures to gain complete ascendency over me. I had always owned them to be the Word of God . . . the careful reading of Acts afforded me a practical picture of the early church; which made me feel deeply the contrast with its actual present state. . . ." *Letter to Prof. Tholuck,* as quoted by Neatby, *op. cit.,* pp. 35-36.

Wicklow as a clergyman and I was still going to Stanford Chapel."[14] The resignation may safely be assigned to the latter part of 1828 or early 1829. His churchmanship does not seem to have ended, however, with his resignation but to have continued until as late as 1834 when Bellett inferred that he was "all but detached from the Church of England."[15]

An analysis of these early days reveals that the first meetings were spontaneous gatherings of men with kindred minds, and were not protest meetings at all. The principles which later infused the entire Brethren movement were, however, gradually growing upon the consciousness of the men involved.

Another nonconformist movement was growing in Dublin at about the same time, which was later to amalgamate with the first. The leader of this group was Edward Cronin, a convert from Catholicism who came to Dublin in 1826 as a medical student. As an Independent he was admitted to fellowship with several dissenting societies for a while, but was later refused admission to any of them until he definitely aligned himself with one of them. It is clear that Cronin's mind had been moving in channels similar to that of Groves, for he remarks, "This left me in separation from the table for several months . . . feeling unable to attend their meetings from the growing opposition to a one-man ministry."[16]

This move resulted in a protest by Edward Wilson, assistant secretary to the Bible Society, and to his subsequent withdrawal from the Society. With Wilson, two of his cousins, and a fifth member, Cronin started a group in his house on Lower Pembroke Street, where they, paralleling the group attended by Groves, Bellett, and Darby, emphasized the principle of oneness of the assembly before God, and the liberty of ministry in Christ.

There is some confusion about how the two groups amalgamated. Darby indicates that Cronin's group had disbanded, and that "five of us — Bellett, Cronin, Hutchinson, Master Brooks . . . and myself met together at Hutchinson's house in Fitzwilliam Square."[17] According to Cronin, however, his

14. A. G. Bellett, *Recollections of J. G. Bellett*. London: G. Morrish, n.d., p. 24.
15. *Loc. cit.*
16. Edward Cronin, as quoted by Neatby, *op. cit.*, p. 19.
17. J. N. Darby, *Account of Proceedings*, p. 187.

group did not dissolve, but expanded considerably, so that they were joined by Frances Hutchinson, "who, as we were becoming so numerous . . . offered us the use of his large room in Fitzwilliam Square."[18] Bellett more or less corroborates Cronin's account:

> In the summer of 1829 our family was at Kingstown and dear Francis Hutchinson at Bray. We saw each other occasionally and spoke of the things of the Lord. . . . on returning to Dublin . . . Hutchinson was quite prepared for communion in the name of the Lord with all . . . who loved Him in sincerity, and proposed to have a room in his house in Fitzwilliam Sq. for that purpose. . . . Cronin was prepared for this fully. . . . Thus we continued from November, 1829.[19]

Opinions expressed at this meeting again disclose that among certain of the leaders there still remained an attachment to the Established Church.

> At this time J. G. Bellett and J. N. Darby were more or less affected by the general state of things in the religious world but were unprepared to come out into entire separation. They looked suspiciously at our movement, feeling still able to attend and minister in the Church of England, as well as to come occasionally to our little assembly.[20]

Bellett concurs by commenting, "I joined, but I do not think with the same liberty and decision of mind."[21] This hesitancy was due in part, no doubt, to the fact that until this time the meeting had not become a publicly announced dissenting group. Hutchinson apparently had no thought of establishing such a group when he extended the invitation to meet in his house, for Bellett recalls that "he did so, designing however so to have it, that if any were disposed to attend services in the parish church, or the dissenting chapels, they might not be hindered . . . ."[22]

Whatever were the intentions of the leaders, such a group evolved from the room in Fitzwilliam Square, for it became both a permanent and regular place of meeting. Six months later the group moved to a public location on Aungier Street,

18. Cronin, as quoted by Neatby, *op. cit.*, p. 20.
19. Bellett, *op. cit.*, p. 21.
20. Cronin, as quoted by Neatby, *op. cit.*, p. 20.
21. Bellett, *op. cit.*, p. 26.
22. *Loc. cit.*

meeting in a hired hall.[23] The move was prompted by increased numbers and the proposal to let the breaking of bread
become more of a witness.[24] This was the first public announcement of services, and as such, Brethrenism as a public
movement was born.

> . . . the consolidating force of the movement issued from the com-
> pany that finally gathered at Aungier St. . . . Brethrenism was in-
> deed formed out of a variety of little meetings of a more or less
> similar character, and these must be accepted as its ultimate ele-
> ments; but Brethrenism, as we know it, is a synthesis, and the
> synthesis has a history; and I do not believe that its history can
> truly be told without locating its original force in Dublin, and at
> Aungier St.[25]

When the meetings began in Hutchinson's house in 1829 he
"prescribed a certain line of things, as the service of prayer,
singing and teaching, that should be found amongst us each
day."[26] When the move to Aungier Street was made, however,
the settled order of worship observed at Fitzwilliam Square
was gradually abandoned. Teaching and exhortation were
made common duties and services, and prayer, which had been
restricted to two or three elders, became free to all when elder-
ship ceased to be recognized. It gradually became the law of
Brethrenism to disown all regularly constituted authority, all
predetermined arrangement, and all prudential provision, even
for emergencies which might arise.[27]

The only conditions for admission into the fellowship were
a simple faith in Christ and a consistent walk in Christian
love. All who felt themselves fitted to edify, and who were
regarded by the assembly as acceptable teachers, were at liberty
to address the group. The Brethren insisted on a spiritual
ministry, and believed that they were returning to the original
principles of ministry. For the same reason they did not

23. Not without some dissension on the part of the leaders who had
strong ties with the Established Church. "Bellett was adverse to the
change; Hutchinson was reluctant; Darby was absent; Cronin and Stokes
(as nonconformists) were eager for it . . ." Neatby, *op. cit.*, p. 22. This
is but further evidence that the protest element was not primary in the
beginning of the movement.

24. Miller, *op. cit.*, p. 21.

25. Neatby, *op. cit.*, p. 24.

26. Bellett, *op. cit.*, p. 30.

27. Neatby, *op. cit.*, p. 38.

organize any church.[28] The principles of breaking of bread every Lord's Day, the unity of all saints in Christ, and the freedom of the Holy Spirit to work among them were paramount features of their worship. A common expression among the leaders of this period was "the Blood of the Lamb, and the Union of the Saints."[29]

The early meetings have been described as

> . . . fellowship with those who . . . assembled upon principles taught in the Word of God, where no sectarian walls of division was acknowledged, and where there was liberty of the Spirit of God to minister to the truths (sic) of the Scripture by those who were gifted by Him for that purpose.
>
> The distinction between poor and rich was lessened by holy, loving fellowship and unity. . . .Their dress was plain, their habits simple and their walk distinguished by separation from the world. The meetings of the assembly were calm, peaceful and hallowed; their singing soft, slow and thoughtful; their worship evinced the nearness of their communion with the Lord; their prayers were earnest for an increased knowledge of God, and the spread of his truth. Their teaching showed their deep searching of the Scripture under the guidance of the Holy Spirit, while the exercise of the varied ministry, under the power of the Holy Spirit, testified to the blessedness of the teaching of God's Word on each important subject. . . .
>
> I breathed what appeared to me to be the pure element of love. . . . I was enlightened by its teachings, cheered by its joys, comforted by its hallowed fellowship, strengthened by godly companionship, and encouraged by those who were over me in the Lord. . . . The fruits of the Spirit were in evidence.[30]

It is doubtful whether Darby was a real leader in this Dublin meeting, for there seems to be little reference to any marked contribution which he made. He attended the meetings and approved their principles, but he does not seem to have been permanently located in Dublin. In relating the first meeting at Fitzwilliam Square, he adds, "I afterwards went down and

---

28. J. N. Darby, *Narrative of Facts Connected with the Separation of the Writer from the Congregation Meeting in Ebrington Street*, Col. Writ., Eccl. Vol. IV, p. 136.

29. Neatby, *op. cit.*, p. 39.

30. W. H. Cole, unpublished letter as quoted by David J. Beattie, *The Brethren, The Story of a Great Recovery*, Kilmarnock, John Richie, Ltd., 1939, pp. 19-20; G. H. Lang, *The Local Assembly*, Walsham-le-Williows, author, 1942, Appendix A, p. 72. While the description given above refers primarily to the Plymouth meeting, it is characteristic of the movement in the early days.

worked at Limerick."[31] Consequently, he was not in Dublin when the decision to move to Aungier St. was made.

From Limerick he went to Oxford "after July, 1830," where he was associated with George Wigram, where "breaking of bread had already begun."[32] Subsequently he met B. W. Newton, who invited him to Plymouth. With Wigram, Newton, and a Captain Hall who had been preaching in the villages, "reading meetings were held, and the following year, 1831, began the practice of breaking of bread."[33] There was a group meeting with Newton before Darby arrived, but it remained for him to establish the principles which marked it as a continuation of the Dublin movement.

It was at Plymouth that the name "Brethren" was first used in connection with the group in England. Darby objected to denominational names, believing them to be at variance with the New Testament. He referred to the practice of Jesus and the apostles of addressing the believers as "brethren," "holy brethren," and "beloved brethren," hence the name "brethren" became the designation of the group. The movement at Plymouth grew rapidly so that by 1840 there were 800 attending the meeting.[34] Reference to the movement came to be "the Brethren at Plymouth," and the name "Plymouth Brethren" became an almost inevitable designation for the movement in England. In Ireland it was known as "Darbyism," due, no doubt, to the large influence of his work there after his labors in Plymouth.

Many groups were formed in other parts of Britain. Most notable of these was the one at Bristol where George Müller, brother-in-law of A. N. Groves, and Henry Craik, who had been a tutor in the Groves family, were the guiding forces. This group seems to have been begun entirely independent of the Dublin or Plymouth groups, but came to embody the same

31. Darby, *Narrative of Facts*, p. 136.

32. *Loc. cit.*

33. S. P. Tregelles, *Three Letters to the Author of 'A Retrospect of Events That Have Taken Place Amongst the Brethren.'* London: Houlston & Sons, 1894, 2nd edition, p. 7.

34. W. G. Turner, *John Nelson Darby*, p. 47. James Grant, *The Plymouth Brethren: Their History and Heresies,* London: W. H. Guest, 1876, p. 8, gives the number as 1200-1400 by 1833. He is in error here, however, for most conservative estimates of Brethrenism place that figure as late as 1845.

principles, and was consequently known as belonging to the Brethren movement. Two groups met in Bristol: the Bethesda group, where membership was restricted to those who had been immersed, and Gidson, where membership was open to all. In the summer of 1837, however, both groups united under the principle of open membership.

Under Darby's energetic leadership and influence, Brethren groups were formed with increasing rapidity. The appeal of Brethrenism was one to spiritual unity and freedom, based on a literal interpretation of the Scriptures. The new movement demanded that deeds coincide with creeds, and a revival of personal spirituality grew as the result.

> Men's minds were most unsettled on religious subjects, and many of the best men in the Church of England had left, and were leaving, because of the all but total absence of spiritual life, blended with no small amount of unsound teaching, in it. The result was that many spiritually minded people . . . were in a condition to embrace doctrines and principles of Church government which they considered to be more spiritual than those which were in ascendency in the Establishment.[35]

High among the conditions favoring the rise of Brethrenism was the distinguished social position and intellectual capabilities of its earliest leaders, who were men of considerable gifts, moral prestige, and intelligence — clergymen, barristers, solicitors, military and naval officers, physicians, and men of high title and property.[36] Dominating all these stood the genius of J. N. Darby, who either by design or by sheer force of personality exercised tremendous influence over all meetings.

35. Grant, *op. cit.*, p. 5
36. C. H. Mackintosh, as quoted by Beattie, *op cit.*, p. 16; Thomas Croskery, "John Nelson Darby," *The Catholic Presbyterian Magazine*, VII: 442 (1882). Among these leaders were George Wigram, one of the editors of the *Englishman's Hebrew and Chaldee Concordance*, and a cognate concordance of the Greek New Testament; S. P. Tregelles, outstanding biblical scholar and textual critic; George Müller, founder of one of Britain's most famous orphanages, Ashley Downs; Lord Congleton (John Parnell) ; Sir Alexander Campbell; Lady Powerscourt; the Earl of Craven; F. W. Newman; B. W. Newton, sometime fellow at Oxford; Andrew Miller, prominent church historian, author of *Short Papers on Church History;* W. H. Kelly, author of a critical edition of *The Revelation,* which Professor Henrich Ewal of Göttingen declared was the finest piece of English work of that kind he had ever seen; J. E. Howard, eminent quinologist, a fellow of societies on the continent, as well as in Britain; J. C. Deck, noted hymn writer; and J. S. Oliphant, Director of Funds for the India

In 1838 Darby began his work in Switzerland, where for seven years he enjoyed tremendous successes during his periodic visits. On his return to Britain in 1845 he went to Plymouth, where B. W. Newton had continued to minister since the inception of the society. Within a short time an inevitable strife between the two arose and blossomed into a bitter controversy that did much to stamp the future character of Brethrenism.

Cause for this controversy appears to have been both theological and ecclesiastical, with strong evidence of personality clashes as well. The responsibility for the strife has been much disputed, depending upon the viewpoint of the various writers, but all agree about its result: Where harmony had heretofore reigned, contention was now the rule. A movement which began with the slogan "The Blood of the Lamb and the Union of the Saints" now became a place of controversy about minute theological issues. The communion of the saints, with perfect liberty in Christ replacing ecclesiastical authority, ended in excommunication of the saints.

Darby's account[37] differs somewhat from most of the others.

Office, Foreign Office. Authority for the position and social rank of the above-mentioned may be found in Napoleon Noel, *The History of the Brethren* (Denver: W. F. Knapp, 120 W. Maple Ave, 1936), *passim*.

In his Swiss campaign, Darby admitted that it passed for an aristocratic movement. J. J. Herzog, *Les Freres de Plymouth et John Darby*, p. 82. One of his most severe critics admits, "This circumstance attributed to no small part of its influence." William Reid, *Plymouth Brethrenism Unveiled and Refuted* (Edinburgh: J. B. David, 1893), p. 162.

An interesting commentary on Darby's doctrine, from which dispensationalism stems, is that when his doctrinal divergence from the historic faith began fully to be evident most of these early leaders either disassociated themselves from him or were excommunicated because of their opposition to him.

37. Darby, *Narrative of Facts*, p. 2. This *Narrative*, when compared with other proved reliable sources, such as S. P. Tregelles and A. N. Groves, contains some glaring misstatements. Darby obviously makes the best case possible for his own position. In all fairness to him, however, it must be acknowledged that William Trotter, *The Whole Case of Plymouth and Bethesda*, London, Gospel Book Store, Paternoster Sq., 1849, p. 31, records a meeting at Bath in May, 1848 in which "over 100 Brethren from all parts" subjected the *Narrative* "to strictest scrutiny; Lord Congleton endeavoring for five hours to prove them false. The result was . . . these pamphlets were fully established . . . They were vindicated from every attempt to call their statement in question . . ." However, no other record of the results of this meeting is to be found in the writers

He makes two general charges against Newton: theological error, and enforcing his authority on the assembly. He maintains that he resisted Newton purely out of jealousy for the cause of Christ, not for personal reasons. He asserts that from the very beginning of the movement at Plymouth, Newton had exercised too much power; that he had attempted to warn him of the subsequent effect it would have on the assembly, but that Newton had persisted in usurping the position for selfish aggrandizement.[38]

Darby evidently saw what he terms "the rising tides of clericalism" in the practice concerning the Lord's table, in which the speakers for the table always broke the bread and became recognized as leaders. Newton had become the leading brother, according to Darby, and when he returned, Newton resented his presence.

Darby charges that Newton did not want to co-operate with the other leaders; did not allow the other teachers to attend his meetings because he did not think it right for the taught to hear the authority of the teachers questioned; would not attend general "prophetic" meetings in Ireland, but set up his own meetings in Plymouth at the same time; and, in general, tried to isolate himself from the other brethren.

> . . . I sorrowed over [this] as an unhappy trait of isolation, and the love of acting alone, and having his followers to himself; but I had no suspicion whatever of any purpose of any kind, bore with it as a failing of which we all have some, and left perfect liberty complete and entirely unentrenched on.[39]

---

of this period. All attempts to be objective must hold Trotter's testimony in abeyance until corroborated, since he is obviously determined to justify Darby, and his volume contains many prejudiced statements and, at times, false conclusions.

38. Darby must take at least a partial responsibility for his departure from the original principle of Brethrenism, for in earlier days he had urged Newton to "sit where he could hinder what was manifestly unprofitable and unedifying." Thomas Stewart Veitch. *The Story of the Brethren Movement* (Edinburgh: Pickering and Inglis, n.d.), p. 43. Darby addressed a letter to Newton from Dublin as "B. Newton, Esq. Elder of the Saints meeting at Raleigh Street, Plymouth." Tregelles, *op. cit.*, p. 7. It is apparent even that on one occasion, when Darby was present, Newton stopped a brother from ministry that he considered improper, apparently with Darby's full concurrence. Tregelles, *ibid.*, p. 8.

39. Darby, *Narratives of Facts*, p. 21.

Some of the practices to which Darby objected were the custom of set days for certain speakers — violating the principle of the freedom of the Spirit to "exercise" a man to speak — to the point that the people "knew when it was Mr. Newton's day or Mr. Harris's day"; the outright denial of someone's speaking privilege by pulling him down, scraping of feet, or leaving; the silence of the assembly when some brother would call out a hymn — all of which seemed to him to be a deliberate attempt on the part of Newton to control the assembly. The first evidence of strife between the two appears to be over a doctrinal issue concerning the status of the church during the Great Tribulation. Darby taught that the entire Christian church would be raptured, and the witness during the tribulation would be borne by a semi-Christian group, who, though not a part of the church, would be under a form of grace. He distinguished between the church (Pentecost to rapture) and the saints of the Old Testament, asserting that the church had a special glory and that the Old Testament saints had an inferior relationship to God. To explain the witness of the last days, as set forth in the Gospels, he taught that this was given to the apostles, not as the founders of the church, but as the representatives of the faithful remnant in the midst of an apostate Judaism. This involved a different view of the Gospels than was commonly held, and led to the practice of distinguishing certain parts of them as being "Jewish."

Newton, on the other hand, taught that the "faithful" who were to be persecuted were simply the members of the church who would be on the earth at the time of the tribulation, and that the Old Testament saints were an integral part of the church, there being no "special glory" for the post-Pentecostal saints.

Here is tangible evidence that the dichotomy between Israel and the church was forming in the thought of Darby, growing out of a rigidly applied principle of interpretation. The pre-tribulation rapture, compartmentalizing of Scripture, Jewish nature of the kingdom, all of which have become integral parts of the dispensational system, are clearly present in this conflict.

Newton's view illustrates the contrast between the basic dispensational principle and the concepts which were commonly held at that time. Newton reflected the historic premillennial position. The controversies which were precipitated by this issue formed the pattern of many which were to follow in the struggle between rising dispensationalism and the historic faith.

The doctrinal disagreement resulted in Darby's charging Newton with sectarianism. Darby charged that Newton had contrived to band together many of the Brethren over which he could exercise control and that he had usurped the power of "chief elder," a practice which he felt contrary to the principle of liberty in the Spirit, upon which Brethrenism was founded. The matter was precipitated when Darby returned to Plymouth from a deputation and was greeted coldly by Newton who, after a brief personal call, wrote a letter stating that he would walk "peacefully, but separately."[40]

Darby replied to Newton's letter by objecting to his "having acted very badly toward many beloved brethren, and in the sight of God."[41] Newton requested dates and names, to which Darby replied that the practice of denouncing brethren was pure sectarianism. Newton answered (sarcastically, according to Darby) that this constituted a new charge and that he still wanted names and dates.[42] Darby declined further communication unless it was before the assembled brethren. Newton refused to meet what he termed a "jury," but agreed to meet informally with a selected number of the leading brethren, half of whom Darby could choose. Darby agreed to meet, but refused to select any adherents, asserting this to be unscriptural.

When called upon to state his objections, Darby demurred, but when pressed, he charged "a systematic effort to form a sect, and, discrediting and denouncing those who do not adopt the opinions which form its basis."[43]

40. Darby, *Narrative of Facts*, p. 22; *Account of Proceedings*, p. 159, f.n. Newton later insisted that he was no sectarian, but had come to his conclusion because he disagreed doctrinally with Darby's eschatology.

41. *Loc. cit.*

42. Darby considered this facetious inasmuch as Newton's effrontery in refusing to greet many brethren was widely known. "He had been writing for six years to every part of the globe . . . sisters had been employed in copying these letters; tracts had been published, declaring all that subverted the first element of Christianity." Darby, *Narrative of Facts*, p. 30. (It would be interesting to know what Darby meant by "the first elements.")

43. Darby, *Narrative of Facts*, p. 33.

> Mr. Newton broke out in a great anger, saying that he waived all
> formal objection, that he did seek to make a focus of Plymouth, and
> that his object was to have union in testimony there against the
> other brethren . . . and that he trusted to have at least Devonshire
> and Somersetshire under his influence for that purpose.[44]

Darby stated that if this was true, and it remained unjudged
by the assembly, he did not feel that he could worship with
them the next Lord's Day. Newton replied that he had no
right to do so.

Two meetings after this produced nothing but fresh strife
and contention, quibbling about whether Newton had referred
to specific geographical areas, and whether he had said *a* purpose, or *the* purpose. The other brethren urged Darby not to
press the charge, to which he agreed, and continued ministering for a while.

Darby later went to Somersetshire; J. L. Harris, who had
supported him in his charge against Newton, went to Ireland;
and Newton remained in Plymouth, where, according to Darby,
he taught that there should be recognized teachers. Darby
returned to Plymouth and ministered until Harris, returning
from Ireland, protested about Newton's letters against the Irish
brethren, at which time the party spirit was revived and Darby
ceased ministering until it died down. He attempted to revive
a Friday meeting,[45] but without success. After several attempts
to settle the difficulty proved unavailing, on October 26 Darby

> . . . detained the assembly and told them that it was a matter of
> deepest sorrow, but that I was going to quit the assembly; I felt it
> impossible to enter into details. It would have been a string of
> miserable facts . . . . I therefore refrained from them entirely, and
> only stated the principles on which I went; and more particularly,
> that there was subversion of the principles on which we met; that

44. *Loc. cit.* This is Darby's account, which we may be expect to be
biased.
45. This was a meeting in which the mundane affairs relating to the
work of the assembly had been informally discussed by the brethren, and
which had, in earlier days, served as a "spiritual clearing-house" for the
business and discipline of the assembly. Darby charges that Newton had
suppressed this meeting because it interfered with his quest for authority.
Whether Newton deliberately suppressed it cannot be proved, but the group
ceased to meet some months before the strife began.

there was evil and unrighteousness unconfessed and unjudged I
then left the assembly.[46]

After this action other of the leaders ceased ministering.
Darby was requested to come before the whole assembly to
state in detail why he had left. He records that Newton employed many friends and followers to make a canvass of the
members of the assembly at their homes, urging them not to
attend the meeting, making false issues and malicious statements about him, but that between two and three hundred
people came. "I stated my reasons, and I can truthfully say,
with the presence of the Lord and in grace toward all, I
brought no accusation against Mr. Newton . . . ."[47]

Later several of the leaders sent a note to Darby requesting
him to appoint four of his followers to meet four of Newton's
to examine the charges. Darby refused on the ground that such
procedure was not scriptural, and that the matter should be
brought before the entire assembly. Newton then gathered a
group of partisans at his home to give his side of the division;
this meeting has become known as the "meeting of the ten."

Darby asserts that this was entirely without dependence
upon the Spirit, citing the fact that the group was composed of
men who were known to be followers of Newton; that one man,
a Mr. N-r, whose loyalty to Newton was in question, was barred
from the meeting. He accused Newton of threatening "to produce in every gathering united hostility to the brethren's teaching who differed from him on points which were discussed."[48]

When some of the brethren wanted to bring the charges
before the assembly, they were told by Newton that the assembly had no authority to judge; that it was absurd for the
untrained, the poor, to sit in judgment upon the teachers.
Darby waited for the proposed meeting to be called, but when

46. Darby, *Narrative of Facts,* p. 60. Eight years later, Darby acknowledged that his action may have been hasty in one respect. He
admits that had he waited to see what effect the announcement of Harris
(that he would no longer minister at Plymouth) would have on the
assembly, his actions might have been different. In every other respect,
he positively affirms that he has no regrets for his act. J. N. Darby, *Letter
of Acknowledgement as to Plymouth,* November 23, 1853, Col. Writ., Eccl.
Vol. IV, pp. 308-10.

47. Darby, *Narrative of Facts,* p. 62; *Account of Proceedings,* p. 224.

48. Darby, *Narrative of Facts,* p. 73. If this statement is true, Darby
must have heard it from another, for he was not present at the meeting.

it did not come, decided to break all connections with the Ebrington Street meeting (the meeting at Plymouth to which Newton was attached), and to set up his own "table."

> I hesitated whether I should demand Raleigh St. and do it as a public testimony; but praying over it I felt the humble and more gracious way would be to do it for my own need. I procured a small room, knowing about six who wished to do it, for I had most carefully avoided seeking any, and had eventually ceased visiting, lest I should have the appearance of making a party . . . .
> I began to break bread, and the first Sunday there were not six, but sixty.[49]

This happened on December 28, 1845.

Darby's account of the events leading to the division places the responsibility almost entirely on Newton. A close examination of the facts, however, will suggest that Darby was partially at fault. The accusation that Newton attempted to gain personal authority over the assembly is supported by Newton's own admission, by the testimony of others,[50] and by the facts. However, Darby's action precipitated additional strife after the original division and set the pattern for continual division and strife among the Brethren long after Newton had retired from the scene.

Darby was not guiltless of the very thing which he charged to Newton, as may be seen from the testimony of Groves, who contends that Darby was "pained and disappointed that Newton's influence was paramount in Plymouth"; that his position was "painful . . . since he was bent on ruling" when an undisguised partisanship placed him in the minority.[51]

---

49. Darby, *Narrative of Facts,* p. 78.

50. S. P. Tregelles, *Five Letters To The Editor of "The Record."* London: Houlston and Wright, 1864, 2nd edition, p. 16. Of all the biographers of the early days of Brethrenism, Tregelles is without a doubt the most reliable, though brief. His personal integrity to facts, in addition to his outstanding scholarship, makes him an almost unimpeachable source.

51. Groves, *op. cit.,* p. 32. Groves may be classed with Tregelles regarding his integrity as an honest reporter. Never a partisan of either faction, he had earlier indicated his displeasure at Darby's tendency to dominate. As early as March 10, 1836, after spending fifteen months on furlough from his labors in the mission work of India, he wrote Darby counselling against the practice of taking chief place of judgment over the assemblies. This letter is significant in that it shows that this tendency was present in Darby long before the incident of division, and it prophetically predicts the course of action to be taken by Darby and Brethrenism. Of

The strife continued throughout the following year. On January 11, 1846, Lord Congleton publicly accused Wigram at the Rawstrone Street meeting (in London) of assisting Darby in an unwarranted act of dividing the Plymouth meeting, admitting that a sectarian and clerical spirit existed, but that the division was not necessary. No action was taken, and he ceased breaking bread with them "because they did not do all they could to prevent division."[52]

In April Congleton attended a meeting of the brethren "from other parts" in Rawstrone St. and again publicly charged

> . . . that Mr. Darby, after withdrawing from communion, Sunday, October 26, 1845, giving certain reasons, did publicly slander and defame, in Ebrington Street, Monday, November 17, 1845, his neighbor, his Christian brother and fellow minister in the Word, and thereby caused a breach and division in that gathering.[53]

Again no action was taken. In the weeks that followed continued accusations were brought against Newton by Darby and Wigram. Most significant of these was that a spirit of delusion from Satan was working at Plymouth. The spirit in which the controversy was carried out is indicated by Tregelles, who remarks, "This led to the course of action carried on against him by Mr. Darby and his associates, at first privately . . . then publicly. When all efforts to traduce the character of Mr. Newton had failed . . ."[54]

> Newton came to London to conduct some Bible readings and stated that his errand to town was partly to meet any brethren who were wishful of information as to the charges brought against him in the *Narratives of Facts* . . . The Brethren to whom Mr. Newton had offered to give information proposed to him this open investigation.[55]

A letter was sent requesting Newton to come to Rawstrone

Groves' integrity, Neatby, *op. cit.*, p. 65, declares, "Groves . . . with his singularly pure, lofty and tender spirit . . . was essentially catholic, and he had to endure the grief . . . which to a man less pure from the taint of self-seeking would have been the bitter mortification of seeing another man enter into his labors and convert them to purposes that he abhorred."

52. Neatby, *op. cit.*, p. 122.
53. *Ibid.*
54. Tregelles, *Five Letters*, p. 16.
55. Trotter, *op. cit.*, p. 14

Street to answer Darby's charges. He answered that he would be pleased to meet with any of the brethren, naming the hour and the date. Joseph B-r, answering for the brethren at Raw-strone Street, wrote,

> The object of the note sent to you from the ten brethren yesterday was not to request that you meet those who signed it, as your note seemed to infer, but that you state when and where you intended to meet the saints publicly . . . and to which they request a direct reply.56

Newton replied that the meeting of the ten had exonerated him, that the assembly at Plymouth had issued a similar statement,57 and that he did not feel it necessary to answer the charges publicly again.

Darby contends, however, that the decision resulting from the investigation of the ten brethren did not examine the "whole charge" against Newton, for, at the time they met, only two charges had been made.

> I was called on to give my reasons to the saints why I seceded. In doing so I was obliged to state two particular things as to Mr. Newton . . . but I carefully avoided mentioning anything that did not lead to my leaving, and hence mentioned only the two things as charged. . . . Lately . . . I felt bound to give a narrative of what had passed at Plymouth, and in this six or seven failings of the same kind appear, that is, four or five more graver (sic) than the two I already mentioned."58

Accordingly, Newton had not answered all the charges brought against him, and hence the necessity for the proposed Raw-

---

56. Darby, *Account of Proceedings,* p. 127.

57. Newton refers not only to the earlier decision of the meeting of the ten, but to an investigation of four men who were appointed by the assembly at Plymouth. Darby charges, however, that these four men were known partisans and instruments of Newton (Darby, *What Investigation Has Been Made at Plymouth,* Col. Writ., Eccl. Vol. IV, pp. 255-56) ; that none of them were present at Plymouth when the incidents to be investigated were happening — one of them was not converted until years afterwards, the other three did not come to the Plymouth assembly until later (Darby, *Account of Proceedings,* p. 209; *Summary of Meetings in London,* Col. Writ., Eccl. Vol. IV, p. 276, where the statement is attributed to Mr. H. — presumably J. L. Harris) ; and that the assembly merely accepted their decision without further investigation (Darby, *Account of Proceedings,* p. 211) . He further charges that Newton passed over several revered and respected leaders in choosing the four, and this proves that it was not a fair investigation (Darby, *What Investigation . . . ,* p. 256) .

58. Darby, *What Investigation . . . ,* p. 263.

strone St. meeting; Newton's *Defense* having been first published in 1845, while the new charges of Darby's *Narrative of Facts* did not appear until 1846.

A second summons was sent by W. H. Dorman, requesting an immediate reply. W. H. Soltau, answering for Newton, sent a short reply indicating that a more detailed answer would be shortly forthcoming, but that the answer would be another refusal. Without waiting for the lengthy explanation,[59] Dorman informed the assembly that Newton had refused to answer the charges and must therefore accept their guilt; that he, Dorman, would no longer break bread with him.

A third note was directed to Newton to which he gave a most firm and decidedly negative answer as to a formal meeting, but reiterated his willingness to meet with any individual or group of individuals who acted only from the desire to obtain information without pressing formal charges. Consequently, Dorman and Gough signed a note on behalf of the Rawstrone St. assembly formally refusing him fellowship at the Lord's table.[60]

The injustice of this act is illustrated by the fact that Newton had not applied for fellowship at the Rawstrone St. assembly when the summons was first delivered; that the lengthy reply promised in the note by Soltau was never read before the assembly; that the action indicated in the "excommunication" was far from being unanimous;[61] and that the spirit with

59. In a letter to Mr. C-w, Dorman indicated that he could not read the reasons to the assembly. "At my declining, therefore, to read any reasons that may come to me for the saints at Rawstrone St. you must not be grieved, as it is only declining in act what I had already done by letter" (Darby, *Account of Proceedings*, p. 135). When called on to read the reasons in a later meeting, Dorman refused to do so, stating that they did not satisfy him (*ibid.*, p. 138). In a letter to the leaders at Plymouth, Dorman and Henry G-h (possible Gough) wrote, ". . . we beg to say that many of the Statements are so entirely untrue, and its perversion regarding the course of action in question so very sad, that, for ourselves, we do not think that it would be the path of godly wisdom to read it to the saints . . ." (*ibid.*, p. 234; Letter dated Dec. 22, 1846 and Jan. 8, 1847, *ibid.*, p. 247).

60. The letter made it plain that the "congregation at Rawstrone Street do not express any judgment on the matter charged, but simply on the fact of your refusal." Darby, *Account of Proceedings*, p. 142.

61. Even Darby admits that some who were present protested against the move.

which it was conducted was that of tenacious prosecution, not of a humble search for the Lord's will.[62] On this ground, Tregelles wrote a letter to the assembly in "protest against the character, objects, and competency for disciplinary action of the meeting . . . as being wholly contrary to the Word of God, and the authority of our Lord Jesus Christ."[63]

A doctrinal aspect was added to the strife when two specific instances combined to give the Darbyites much ground for attacking Newton. The first charge, in 1846, grew out of some incorrect notes taken by a listener of an address by Newton on Psalm 6. These notes, not taken in shorthand, came into the possession of J. L. Harris, one of Darby's chief supporters. Without communicating with Newton to ascertain the validity of the notes, Harris wrote a tract severely attacking the doctrinal position indicated by them.

The gist of Newton's position was that Christ, as a man and an Israelite, took upon Himself the imputation of Adam's sin, and was therefore under wrath; that by obedience in this life He delivered himself from the wrath, and could thereby become the sacrifice for all men. He denied, as he was charged, that Christ's suffering on the cross was for His own atonement. His chief mistake seems to have been an overzealous desire to identify Christ's humanity in every way with that of man.

Before replying to Harris's tract, Newton issued one of his own, *Remarks on the Suffering of the Lord Jesus,* in which he set forth his own position "repudiating ever having held the heretical doctrines, and fully vindicated himself of the charges thus unjustly imputed to him, but his enemies only took occasion therefrom to increase their accusations."[64] The injustice of Harris's tract, called a "work of darkness" by Müller, may be seen in the statement of Newton.

> I never saw one line of these notes, nor indeed knew of their existence . . . until I heard that they were read and severly censured in a meeting convened in Exeter for that purpose. Shortly afterwards they were published, accompanied by strictures. . . . This was done without any communication having been made to me, and therefore no opportunity was afforded me of avowing or

62. Neatby, *op. cit.,* p. 128.
63. *Ibid.*
64. Tregelles, *Three Letters,* p. 8.

disavowing any of the sentiments, or of rendering any explanation, or even of giving any judgment as to the accuracy of the notes.[65]

Darby replied with two tracts, *Observations by J. N. D. on a Tract Entitled, "Remarks on the Suffering of the Lord Jesus,"* and *A Plain Statement of Doctrine on the Sufferings of Our Blessed Lord,* in which he uses expressions such as "hopeless dishonesty of author," "subverts the faith," "an affinity to Arianism," "Mr. Newton received his prophetic system by direct inspiration from Satan, analogous to the Irvingite delusion," "entire indifference to the truth and glory of Christ," "fatal error slurred and glossed over," "fatal ignorance of essential truth," and "seducing spirit."

Newton published another tract, *A Statement and Acknowledgement Respecting Certain Doctrinal Errors,* in which he asserted,

> I wish to explicitly state that I do not ascribe any of Christ's living experience to the imputation of Adam's guilt, nor ought I to have made any statement or used any words which . . . ascribe any of this suffering to anything imputed to Him; not yet that He had by keeping the law or by anything else to deliver Himself from such imputation or its consequences.[66]

Darby and his supporters considered this to be only a partial denial of his error, and published a *Notice of the Statement,* in which Darby declared Newton still to be guilty of doctrinal error.[67]

A second charge of doctrinal error was brought against Newton soon after the first. In 1835 he had published a pamphlet against Irvingism, defending Christ's spotless humanity, but in which some of the relations in which our Lord stood to others were inaccurately set forth. In 1847, twelve years later, these statements were eagerly seized by some of his opponents and used against him. When the passages were brought before

---

65. B. W. Newton, *Observations on a Tract,* Plymouth: Wright & Son, p. 4.

66. B. W. Newton, *A Statement and Acknowledgement Respecting Certain Doctrinal Errors,* Plymouth: Wright & Son, 1847, p. 11.

67. "It is to be remembered that this humble document was the work of a distinguished scholar and theologian, a Fellow of Exeter College, Oxford. . . . If it be asked why so thorough a confession and withdrawal did not end the controversy, the answer must be that Mr. Newton's opponents had ceased to walk in love, and therefore carnal influences, such as bitterness, ambition, a party spirit overcame them." G. H. Lang, *The Local Assembly.* Suffolk: The author, 1942, 4th edition, pp. 63, 62.

him he attentively examined them, and realizing that they might well lead to false conclusions he published a statement withdrawing them.

The original pamphlet appeared in the *Christian Witness* of April, 1835, and did not then contain the passages objected to. These passages were inserted *at the request and with the approval of the leaders at Plymouth* in order to meet certain Irvingite errors which had crept in, and the pamphlet containing them reappeared in enlarged form in the second edition of the same magazine in 1838. It had been widely circulated among Brethren circles for twelve years and had been commended by practically all the leaders.[68]   J. G. Bellett, one of the most able of the Darbyites, acknowledged that he had seen nothing wrong with it until the error was pointed out. The most objectionable statement in the article was later proved to be a quotation from Darby, and after this was revealed it was interpreted to mean something quite different.

The statements objected to did not refer to the *person* of Christ, but to certain relations which He had to Adam. Throughout the pamphlet Newton strongly maintained the true deity of Christ, His sinlessness, the purity and holiness of His life, the entire voluntariness of His service and sufferings, and the substitutional character of His work.

> He did not see, neither did the brethren who approved and circulated this pamphlet discover, until after *twelve years* had elapsed, the consequence that might have been deduced from these statements . . . . It is manifest from the pamphlet itself, as well as other writings, that Mr. Newton did not hold the heretical doctrines with which he was charged. He had stated certain views which might have led toward them, and when he saw what might be deduced therefrom, he fully, frankly and publicly acknowledged that he had made an inaccurate statement, and withdrew it. . . . The accusers of Mr. Newton are not to be blamed for pointing out an incorrect statement in one of his early writings . . . but they are open to the severest censure for the bitterness and malice which characterized their accusations, and for attributing to him heretical doctrines which he never held.[69]

Newton's withdrawal of his statement did not end the painful controversy, but placed an instrument of advantage in the

---

68. It was even edited by J. L. Harris, who later brought the charges against Newton for his lecture notes on Psalm 6 (Trotter, *op. cit.*, p. 22) .
69. Tregelles, *op. cit.*, pp. 12-13.

hands of his opponents, who used it as an admission of heresy and referred to it as "mere cunning device," "the clever expediency of the enemy of souls in bringing about that which he can use to cloak our sins and blasphemy."[70] This merely increased the intensity of the campaign against Newton.[71]

Newton subsequently left Plymouth, completely disassociated himself from the Brethren, and went to London, where he became the sole pastor of a congregation until his health caused him to retire.

The effect of the controversy did not end with his departure, however. As soon as he left Plymouth, Soltau, Balten, Dyer, Haffner, and others of his associates confessed to clericalism and to unconscious doctrinal errors, and withdrew from the Ebrington Street meeting.[72]

70. *Ibid.*, p. 14.

71. It is not the intention of the author to justify Newton in every respect, but merely to present the facts. There is much in Newton's system that is as decidedly wrong as in Darby's, but on the whole he has been much abused by his opponents, and in all fairness to him it must be pointed out that he was the victim of what was obviously a vicious and deliberate attack, of such a nature that it does no credit to those who launched it.

Neatby adequately expresses the case for Newton when he writes, "The execrations of his adversaries pursued him to his distant grave, but not once in a half century did they avail to provoke retaliation. His name to this day is regarded with absolute loathing by thousands who have never troubled to read a single tract of all he has written; and there are certainly hundreds, scarcely a whit better informed, who have made it one of their chief objects to perpetuate the frantic prejudice. But none of the leaders of this campaign of calumny, and none of their dupes, have ever, so far as I can learn from extensive enquiry, been assailed by Newton with one angry word of a personal character, or with one uncharitable imputation. . . . As I know not where to turn for a parallel to usage so cruel and unrighteous as that from which Newton suffered, so I hardly know better where to turn to match such extraordinary forbearance as he displayed. If theological animosity could still restrain me from recognizing the grace of God in his conduct, I should feel that words were poor to express my admiration either of the dignity with which it was pursued through all its bitter length. It seems to me that Newton ignored, all unwittingly, some of the most sacred principles of Holy Scripture; but the light of one text at least shone steadily on his path. When he was reviled, he reviled not again; when he was persecuted, he threatened not; but committed himself to Him that judgeth righteously." Neatby, *op. cit.*, pp. 152-53.

72. Some of these confessions reveal what Newton's heresy was considered to be. Haffner stated, "The other point which he [Darby] contested, viz, 'The practical denial of the presence of the Holy Ghost in the Church,' existed in Ebrington St., I am also fully assured of; and with

Within a few weeks the assembly at Ebrington Street met to draw up a statement of the position of the congregation regarding the error with which they had been connected.[73] It disavowed any approval of errors concerning the person or nature of Christ, and affirmed in definite and concise terms, probably worded by Dr. Tregelles, the orthodoxy of their own beliefs. This statement is significant in the light of subsequent events concerning the relation of the members of Ebrington Street to other Brethren.

It was not, however, sufficient for the followers of Darby. When a certain Colonel Woodfall moved from Plymouth to Bristol and was received into the fellowship of Bethesda at Bristol, a few of Darby's friends objected on the grounds that Woodfall was a friend of Newton. In the course of a public address at Exeter, Darby announced that he would not worship again at Bethesda because the Woodfalls were received, and later, upon the advice of friends, communicated this decision to Mr. Müller.

The friends of Darby in the assembly at Bethesda agitated for an investigation of Newtonian errors, but the leaders firmly refused to do so. After continued insistence on their

sorrow, and deep abasement, confess my sin for having been unwilling to speak of it heretofore. My assurance of this arises from a conversation I had with Mr. Newton, just before leaving Plymouth, on the subject of *preparation for the ministry;* when he said, that, before coming to the Lord's table, he did not see it at all wrong to be prepared with what he had to say to the saints; that if they were in the right state, he believed *that* was the way God by His Spirit (the saints waiting on Him, and the teachers waiting on Him also, before coming) would teach, though he would always be subject to having his thoughts turned into another channel when at the Lord's table, if the Spirit so ordered it. This, beloved friends shocked me very much, at the time, and shook my confidence: but oh! with what humiliation do I now appear in the presence of God, for having so long retained in my bosom the knowledge that our poor brother did thus *practically* deny the *present* leading and guidance of the Spirit of God . . . without having called on others to join with me in prayer for him . . . ." T. P. Haffner, *Confessions,* as quoted by Tregelles, *op. cit.,* p. 30.

73. *A Statement From Christians Assembling in the Name of the Lord in Ebrington Street, Plymouth.* This statement did not satisfy some of the followers of Darby. Wigram answered by declaring of the meeting at Ebrington Street, "Rather would I go to the table of the Socinians or of the Unitarians than to it." J. E. Howard, *A Caution Against the Darbyites,* London: G. T. Stevenson, 1866, p. 36.

part, the assembly was finally called together, and a letter representing the views of ten elders was read. It alleged that the assembly could not consent to an investigation since it was not for the good of the assembly to become entangled in the Plymouth controversy, and that Mr. Newton had repudiated his errors and therefore could not be held to be *presently* responsible for them. They stated,

> Supposing the author of the tracts were fundamentally heretical, this would not warrant us in rejecting those who came from under his teaching, until we were satisfied that they understood and imbibed views essentially subversive of foundation-truths; especially as those meeting at Ebrington St., Plymouth, last January, put forth a statement disclaiming the errors charged against the tracts.[74]

Darby came to Bristol and again urged Müller to begin an investigation, threatening to separate them from all other believers if they refused. When they refused, he issued a circular on August 26, 1848, virtually excommunicating the entire assembly at Bethesda and all other assemblies who received anyone who worshipped at Bethesda.[75]

This letter defined the motive of such action as "guarding the beloved sheep of Christ against the work and power of Satan." It charged that Bethesda's refusal to investigate the Newtonian error was virtually an acceptance of the error inasmuch as it allowed Newton's followers to come into fellowship without regard to their doctrinal beliefs. Darby ignored three salient facts: that Newton had retracted his error; that the assembly at Ebrington Street had asserted that it did not hold such error; and that Bethesda examined each candidate on individual merit. Darby instructs his readers,

> Let this be maintained as I desire to maintain it. . . . I call on brethren by their faithfulness to Christ, and love of souls of those dear to Him, to set a barrier against this evil. Woe be it to them if they love the brethren Müller and Craik or their own case more than the souls of saints dear to Christ! And I plainly urge upon them that to receive anyone from Bethesda . . . is opening the door now to the infection of an abominable evil from which at so much painful cost we have been delivered . . . . If this be admitted by receiving persons from Bethesda, those doing so are

---

74. Henry Groves, *Darbyism, Its Rise and Development,* as quoted by Neatby, *op. cit.,* p. 160.

75. J. N. Darby, *The Bethesda Circular,* Col. Writ., Doc. Vol. IV, p. 253.

> morally identified with the evil . . . . *I shall neither go near*
> *Bethesda in its present state, nor while in that state go where*
> *persons from it were knowingly admitted.*[76]

The effect of this near-decree was almost immediate. Most
of the followers of Darby rejected even normal social contacts
with the Bethesdaites, the division becoming apparent even
within families and close relations.[77] The record of the strife
generated by such a policy shows an appaling degree of dis-
unity among the Brethren everywhere, to the extent that allegiance to the party of Darby or of Müller became the watchword of fellowship, replacing allegiance to Christ.

The pressure on Bethesda was too great, and the leaders
finally yielded in November, 1848, and resolved to examine
Newton's tracts. Seven congregational meetings were held
between November 27 and December 11 at which the tracts
were examined page by page. These deliberations produced
the decision that "no one defending, maintaining, or upholding
Mr. Newton's views or tracts should be received into communion."[78] The decision emphasized that the basis of pro-
hibiting communion was solely adherence to the *doctrine* of
Newton, not merely past association with him. Soon afterwards, however, Bethesda reverted to its earlier decision and
admitted every person who met its own standard of orthodoxy,
irrespective of his ecclesiastical views.

This action did not unite the two factions, for Bethesda still
adhered to its privilege of judging each person on individual
merits rather than past association. The ensuing days produced fresh strife. The Orchard Street assembly of London
declined to comply with the decree that they refuse fellowship
to anyone coming from Bethesda, and were promptly excommunicated. A. N. Groves, returned from his missionary duties
in India, visited a meeting at Totterham. Dorman notified
John Howard, the leading elder at Totterham, that since Groves
was "identified with things at Bethesda."[79] Totterham was
considered excommunicated. As a result of this action Cronin,
who had labored with Groves in unbroken intimacy and

76. Darby, *The Bethesda Circular*, p. 253.
77. Alexander Murdock, *Life Among the Close Brethren*, London:
Hodder and Stoughton, 1890, *passim*.
78. A. N. Groves, *op., cit.*, p. 44.
79. Probably by virtue of the fact that he was Müller's brother-in-law.

friendship for twenty years on the mission field in India, wrote to him and forbade him to enter his house.[80]

The foundation for a permanent division among the Brethren had been laid, a division which was to strip it of much of its virility. The principle of unity and tolerance with which it had begun was replaced by a principle of caustic examination of every theological difference, however minor, until absolute agreement and allegiance to one man was demanded. That man was J. N. Darby.

> In the history of Christendom no man ever entertained so extravagant a conception of sacramental union. If Compton Street [the congregation previously designated as Ebrington St.] admitted Newton to communion, it became as Newton. If Woodfall took communion at Compton Street, he became as Compton Street, and therefore as Newton.
>
> If Bethesda had even excommunicated Woodfall, but had refused to excommunicate one of its own members who had taken communion somewhere else with Woodfall, it would become in the same completeness as Newton. If the Bath meeting, rejecting such a member of Bethesda, had admitted one of the other members to communion, it would have been in Newton's position also; so would Hereford Street, if it had resolved to refuse everyone from Bethesda, but to admit from Bath. To the remotest stage the penalty was exacted. Everyone that took the sacrament at a defaulting meeting was excluded from fellowship.[81]

Subsequently, two groups called Open and Exclusive became clearly distinguished among the Brethren, with Darby dominating the Exclusives.[82]

One of the prime factors in Darby's control of his followers was his establishing of the London Central Meeting, sometimes called London Bridge or "Old Bailey." Observing that the New Testament always referred to *the church* in a given city (e. g., Corinth), Darby concluded that each gathering in a city constituted only a segment of the local church, and could not take ecclesiastical action without the concurrence of the other segments. To facilitate such action he established the

80. Lang, *op. cit.,* p. 27 f.n.
81. Neatby, *op. cit.,* p. 156.
82. The remainder of this historical survey, as well as the analysis of the doctrine of the church and the subsequent evaluation of its contribution, deals only with the Exclusive section of Brethrenism. The reader is cautioned that to attribute all of Darby's doctrine of the church to the Open section would be in error.

Central Meeting, located in a hired room and composed of representatives from the various assemblies of London and suburbs. This meeting met on Saturdays to settle all ecclesiastical problems of London for the following day, such as reception of candidates, details of finance, and excommunication of evildoers or persons who had fellowshipped at an excommunicated assembly. Subsequently, the decisions of the London Central Meeting became binding on the whole of Brethrenism.[83]

An example of the power of this meeting is evidenced in the "Walworth-Sheffield" discipline of 1864. The assembly at Walworth moved its place of meeting to Peckman (becoming known as Walworth-Peckman) without previous permission from the London Central Meeting, and was promptly excommunicated. Subsequently, a member, Goodall, was accepted for fellowship by the Sheffield assembly, which communicated its action to the Totterham assembly. It was excommunicated by that assembly on the ground that it had ignored the decision of the Central Meeting. The wording of the communication, dated November 29, 1863, illustrates the extreme discipline exercised over the various assemblies:

> I am requested to say, that inasmuch as you have now placed yourself in the same position as Mr. G., viz:-outside the communion of the saints gathered in the name of Christ in London, the gathering in Totterham being in fellowship with those in London, cannot receive any statement of the particulars of the matter, either written or by word of mouth. To do so they feel would be to ignore the discipline of the assembly in London, and practically to set aside discipline everywhere; as it virtually denies the unity of the body, and reduces every assembly to an independent congregation.[84]

83. The session became a private one, "sometimes meeting behind closed doors, exercising absolute power, assuming . . . infallibility under the guise of 'the leading of the Holy Ghost.' " (Howard, *op. cit.*, p. 30.) "From this meeting, a weekly paper was issued, ostensibly for the purpose of giving information of the names of persons proposed for and received to fellowship; and also for making known acts of discipline . . . in any of the assemblies it represents. It is symbolic of the unity which belongs to the gatherings where it goes: where it does not go unity is not admitted . . . limiting the unity to the fifteen or sixteen gatherings, and fellowship to the circuit which this paper takes. G. Goodall, *Letters Relating to the Recent Excommunication of Assemblies*. Sheffield: Spurr, 114 West St., n.d., p. 3.

84. Letter dated November 29, 1863, signed C.S. — probably Charles Stanley — as quoted in Howard, *op. cit.*, p. 32.

Darby's comment on the matter, written from the south of France, dated February 19, 1864, shows the absolute sway which he held over his followers for many years.

> . . . He is rejected in London . . . . I take part in this act, and hold him to be outside the church of God on earth, being outside (in either case) what represents it in London . . . . I come to Sheffield; there he breaks bread and is — in what? Not in the church of God on earth, for he is out of it in London, and there are not two churches on earth . . . you have deliberately condemned the gathering in London, and rejected its communion.[85]

Darby's hold over the Exclusive Brethren began to wane with the loss of his chief supporters, either by death or division. By 1865 most of the original group of men who met in Dublin in the early days of Brethrenism had passed from the scene. Groves, Müller, Harris, and Newton had been excommunicated, Bellett and Craik had died, and the ensuing ten years were to bring about more division.

In 1865 two more of Darby's chief supporters, W. H. Dorman and Capt. Hall, withdrew after a lengthy correspondence over Darby's doctrine of the humanity and sufferings of Christ. This doctrine, first developed through the channels of the *Bible Treasury,* was strangely like that for which Darby had condemned Newton. It taught that Jesus was under wrath and indignation, and that He was smitten of God under a "governmental wrath" by which He would have suffered a mortal death had it not been for the cross; it divided the sufferings of Christ into "classes" for various groups of people; and in general, it affirmed the federal imputation of Adam's guilt to Christ — an expression almost identical with that used by Newton.

Dorman wrote to Darby about his doctrine, questioning its orthodoxy.[86] An examination of the correspondence reveals a sincere attempt on Dorman's part to deal in all fairness with Darby. He expresses his devotion for Darby, his good motive in writing, his prayers for Darby's guidance by the Lord. Darby promised to reconsider the matter, but after waiting for months, Dorman became aware that he was not withdraw-

85. Letter addressed to Mr. Spurr, a member of the Sheffield assembly, as quoted in Neatby, *op. cit.,* p. 225.

86. W. H. Dorman, *The Close of Twenty-Eight Years Association With J. N. Darby,* London: Hodder & Stoughton, 1866, 2nd edition, p. 3, *et passim.*

ing, but continually affirming, his doctrine.[87]   Persuading nine of the leaders in London "to sign the whole doctrine [Darby] thus sent it accredited as far as their names could accredit it."[88]

Dorman affirmed a position which he assumed earlier in the correspondence, to wit:

> This is . . . my exact case: I cannot any longer be exposed by the exigency of my position, to be called upon to refuse solicited fellowship to Christians, in other respects upright and blameless, not because they hold Mr. Newton's doctrine, or have the least leaning toward it, but because they cannot abjure all association with those who at some time or other have been connected with Newton's doctrine: — while at the same time more than fear that there is such an approximation of your own doctrine toward it . . . .[89]

Darby's reaction was typical — Dorman was excommunicated, along with Capt. Hall, who shared his view. He attributed their action to the work of Satan.

During the sixties and seventies, the Exclusives experienced a renewed vigor and zest which produced a large influx of new adherents, mostly young men gathered from the Established Church. In 1866 J. E. Howard affirmed, "the sickly existence of Darbyism has been reinvigorated by young blood from the 'revival movement.' "[90]   In 1875 a Scots minister wrote, ". . . they are perhaps increasing even more solidly than any; for their numbers are being constantly augmented by drafts of the most spiritual, intelligent, conscientious, decided, and devoted from all churches . . . ."[91] Among the most outstanding leaders in this movement within Brethrenism were C. H. Mackintosh, Andrew Miller, and Charles Stanley. During most of this period Darby was in deputation work: during the late 1860's he was in Germany, in 1871 in Italy, in 1872 in the U.S.A., in 1875 in New Zealand, and in 1879 on the island of Pau.

---

87. Not only did Darby not withdraw his statement, but in a subsequent tract, stated, "I am not senseless enough to maintain that a pen purely human and feeble may not have expressed itself badly on such subjects, but I see nothing at all to retract from the statements themselves." J. N. Darby, *The Nonatoning Sufferings of Christ*, London: G. Morrish, n.d., p. 2.

88. Dorman, *op. cit.*, p. 19.

89. *Ibid.*, p. 8.

90. Howard, *op. cit.*, p. 34.

91. *Literature and Mission of the So-called Plymouth Brethren*, as quoted in Neatby, *op. cit.*, p. 283.

This influx of new blood into the movement was precisely one of the factors which caused the disintegration of Darby's supremacy over the body, for the new men were not enamored with his doctrines nor under complete sway of his magnetic personality. In the events which followed they felt free to disregard his decrees.

Another factor which contributed to this disintegration was the formation of a party-within-the-party, or New Lumpism, as it was called.[92] The principle tenet of this group was a move for a more "spiritual" element within Brethrenism, bewailing the "increasing worldliness" and advocating admission to the Lord's table only on evidence of "spiritual maturity." It arose primarily as a reaction against the new recruits from the "revival" movement who were not indoctrinated with Brethren doctrine.

Darby resisted this move, for it represented a threat to his supremacy. Subsequent events were to prove that his resistance led to adverse results. It is important to note that at first no new assemblies were formed, and New Lumpism operated within the Exclusive assemblies.

When division did occur, it involved one of the venerable old men of Brethrenism: Dr. Edward Cronin. The assembly at Ryde had long been in Darby's disfavor, since it had refused to judge a member for illegal marriage. A new assembly had been established however, in the home of a young clergyman, a Mr. Finch, a friend of Cronin, who, after leaving the Established Church, had been received by the Brethren in London. When Dr. Cronin went to Ryde, he fellowshipped with his friend in the new assembly; he repeated the act several times in the following weeks and advised the group to transfer its place of meeting to the Masonic Hall. He informed the Kenningston assembly, his regular place of meeting, of this action and communicated it to Darby as well.

On the pretext that this new assembly had not been recognized by the London Central Meeting,[93] a clamor was raised for the excommunication of both it and Dr. Cronin, even though Darby had declared of the old assembly in Ryde, known as Temperance Hall, "Never will I set my foot in that unclean

92. I Corinthians 5:7, "Purge out therefore the old leaven, that ye may be a new lump, as ye are unleavened . . ."
93. Now moved to Cheapside, and known as the Cheapside Meeting.

place. I have known it for twenty years to be a defiled meeting."[94] The London Central intimated to the Kenningston assembly that it would be excommunicated if it did not take action against Dr. Cronin. Darby wrote from Pau, "The course of Dr. Cronin has been clandestine, untruthful, dishonest and profane,"[95] and thereby injected a moral charge into the discussion. Later, on January 5, 1881, he wrote to Cronin to the effect that if he would admit his error he would be restored to favor. Cronin replied, asking whether Darby was prepared to *withdraw,* instead of just drop, the moral charge. Darby's answer made no mention of the charge, and when Cronin replied noticing the omission, the correspondence ceased and the efforts to seek excommunication were pushed relentlessly.

The Kenningston brethren issued a statement on April 28 to the effect that they had no fellowship with Cronin's act or with the assembly he had visited. This was not, however, an act of excommunication, and it was rejected by the Central Meeting. A more formal censure, but still not an excommunication, was passed at Kenningston and rejected at London. After much pressure, on August 19, the Kenningston assembly addressed a letter to "the assembly of God in London" stating,

> After long waiting and prayerful consideration, and the failure of all previous action by the assembly, and admonition, we are sorrowfully compelled to declare Dr. Edward Cronin out of fellowship until he judges and owns the wrongness of his act at Ryde.[96]

For months after, Cronin sat in a back seat in the meeting, out of fellowship, weeping.[97]

The Priory assembly,[98] also known as Park Street, moved to disown fellowship with Cronin, to excommunicate the Kenningston assembly for its failure to judge him without coercion,

---

94. C. Kenswick, *An Explanation of the Principles and Practices of the Park Street Confederacy* (publisher not given), p. 14.

95. J. N. Darby, *Letters of J.N.D.,* London: Stowhill Bible and Tract Depot, n.d., II, 477. It is difficult to find the grounds for such a charge since Cronin had been open in all his actions.

96. G. Balding, *Epitome of the Ramsgate Sorrow. Dates and Facts, with a Few Notes By the Way.* London: G. B. Ferndale Rd., Clapham, Surrey, 2nd. edition, 1882, p. 12.

97. Thomas Stuart Veitch, *op. cit.,* p. 75.

98. Important because it was the assembly at which Darby worshipped when in London.

and the London Central (Cheapside) because it had not taken more definite action. However, Darby suppressed the Priory decision and forced the Central Meeting to accept the Kenningston action.

Peace was not to be restored, however, for the Ramsgate assembly moved to concur in the Priory decision, apart from the disowning of the Central Meeting, and when four of its leaders dissented, others withdrew and formed a separate assembly.[99] Consequently there were two assemblies, the seceders being known as Guildford Hall and the others as Abbott's Hill.

In the months that followed, the Ramsgate question became a source of severe criticism and division. Parties formed rapidly, threatening the complete disintegration of Brethrenism. Darby found himself in disagreement with both groups: with Abott's Hill because it refused to censure Cronin, and with Guildford Hall because, in principle, their seccession threatened to divide his constituency.

The controversy was prolonged through the winter until April, 1881, when Priory (Park Street) and many other assemblies voted to recognize the seceders, Guildford Hall, and notified the Central Meeting to this effect. There is no doubt that the action of the Priory assembly was prompted by Darby, for he had stated that he would leave the Priory if Abbott's Hill were recognized.

On May 8, 1881, Abbott's Hill ceased breaking bread in an effort to form a reunion with Guildford Hall. The latter demanded that each member should make individual application for restoration and confess his sin. Refusing to do this, Abbott's Hill resumed breaking bread on July 12 and the division was irrevocably cemented. As in the Bethesda controversy, recognition of Guildford Hall became the test of fellowship for Brethrenism.

Other assemblies were involved in the controversy of recognizing the decision of Park Street. "Bowing to Park Street" became the criterion for fellowship, even though the principle involved in establishing the Central Meeting decreed that no local assembly had authority. It is important to note that, although Darby levied the threat of total excommunication against all assemblies which did not follow the decision, there

99. Balding, *op. cit.,* pp. 13-15.

were many which did not do so, and openly fellowshipped with Abbott's Hill.

Before 1861 few would have dreamed of defying a Darby edict, but the loss of his chief supporters through death and excommunication, coupled with the influx of new members through the revival of the 1860-70's, had lessened his hold on his constituency, and disintegration was all but complete.

Darby died on April 29, 1882, in his eighty-second year. With his passing the dominating power was lost, and division continued at a rapid rate. Not until the Reunion conferences of 1926 did real unity among the Brethren come into being, when the efforts of many who had long prayed for a restoration of its original unity were realized in part.

No one delights in reviewing the controversies of the church, particularly if they have been characterized by bitter personal incrimination and sharp debate of theological issues. The theological trends that grow out of these controversies are illumined however, by a study of the events and persons involved.

The principles of interpretation of dispensationalism grew out of the Brethren controversies, in spite of any modification they may have undergone since then. John Darby was subjected to the temptations common to all religious innovators — that of constantly advancing new "revelations" of "spiritual" truths to attract and maintain his following. For all of his deep concentration on personal piety, the character of Darby became so warped that, though he may have sincerely desired to interpret the Scriptures accurately, he became absorbed in a system of interpretation which carried him far beyond the historic faith. The history of theology clearly demonstrates that Darby introduced not only new concepts into theology, but a wholly new *principle of interpretation*. He himself admitted that this principle had been hidden from the church for nineteen centuries, and then revealed only to him. One could question seriously whether the framework of thought or the quality of soul of this tortured and confused man provided the proper point of receptivity for a divinely revealed truth.

More important, however, are the implications of the pattern of conduct which he impressed upon his followers. This pattern, rigid and unyielding, formed the defining element of true Christianity and the test for fellowship. It is particularly important to note that nowhere in the controversy was there ever a question about the importance of the new birth, the historicity of the resurrection, the validity of the virgin birth, or any other cardinal doctrine of the Christian faith. The test for fellowship involved less significant points of theology, and more particularly, differences of church *practice*. It is safe to assert that seldom in the history of the church has there been such sharp division over ecclesiastical practice as there was in the Darby movement. The significant thing to note is that these practices grew out of principles of interpretation which form the very essence of dispensationalism, namely, the identification of the blessed hope of the church with a particular chronology of eschatology.

This was a principle of separation. It asserted that where there is no agreement in theology and practice there could be no fellowship. Supposed doctrinal impurities in others demands complete separation of fellowship from them. They are not within the bonds of that "body of Christ" with which fellowship can be held. Separation from evil, said Darby, produces unity in the body of Christ.

One need not scrutinize contemporary evangelical church life too closely to see this principle at work today. Nor does it take more than a casual survey of the history of theology since Darby's day to trace the continuity of his view of separation to our day. There exists a direct line from Darby through a number of channels — prophetic conferences, fundamentalistic movements, individual prophetic teachers, the Scofield Reference Bible, eschatological charts — all characterized by and contributing to a spirit of separatism and exclusion. The devastating effects of this spirit upon the total body of Christ cannot be underestimated.

CHAPTER IV

DARBY'S DOCTRINE OF THE CHURCH

THE TRUE CHURCH, composed of the whole number of regenerate persons from Pentecost to the first resurrection (I Cor. 15:52), who gather in the name of Christ, united together to Christ by the baptism of the Holy Ghost (I Cor. 12:12, 13), is the body of Christ of which He is Head (Eph. 1:22, 23) and the holy temple for the habitation of God through the Spirit (Eph. 2:21, 22). The church exists as God's assembly on the earth,[1] into which the redeemed are gathered as a testimony to God, an inheritance for Christ, and an avenue through which the Holy Ghost works in the heart of man.

The Church in Ruins

From this definition of the nature and purpose of the church, Darby surveys the ecclesiastical scene of his day, both Established and Dissenting, and makes one bold pronouncement: "The Church is in ruins."[2]

The pristine purity of the church as instituted by Christ has become corrupted by the orders and government of man. The universal priesthood of all believers has been usurped by the establishment of professional pastors; uncoverted men are allowed to hold offices which have been instituted by man, not Christ; the presidency of the Holy Spirit has been perverted by man, and in its place believers look to the guidance of a man-made ministry; the bond of communion has been broken; in general, the fellowship which was to reflect the glory of

1. J. N. Darby, *God, Not the Church, the Teacher of His Word*, Col. Writ., Eccl. Vol. IV, p. 361.
2. J. N. Darby, *On the Formation of Churches: Further Developments*, Col. Writ., Eccl. Vol. I, p. 303. This statement is one of the most often asserted in his volumes on Ecclesiology, and one to which he repeatedly turns to answer any argument relative to the church as it exists in governmental form

Christ — simple, direct, Spirit-filled — has been replaced by
a system bearing the evil marks of corrosion:

> Man has organized, but he has wholly set aside, as far as arrange-
> ments go, God's order and arrangements as to the assembly. Thus
> the Church, God's assembly, is set aside to have churches; the Spirit,
> who gives gifts to various members, to have a minister of their
> own choosing; and the Word in which God's order is revealed. The
> Church, Spirit and the Word are all set aside by what is called
> order, that is, man's arrangement and organization.[3]

The church has lost its unity, its power, its holiness, and has
ceased to bear witness to God in the world. What is called
the church has become the center and power of evil and pretense.[4] The members of Christ's body are dispersed: many
are hidden in the world, others in the midst of religious corruption — some in one sect, some in another — in rivalry with
one another.[5]

What is called the church has broken up by its own decrepi-
tude, by the contradictory principles it contains within itself,
and by the absence of all power of self-government.[6] Its ordinances have been perverted, its orders and all spiritual arrange-
ments forsaken and destroyed;[7] outward form and constitution
have superseded spiritual administration,[8] because the church
has forsaken the principles upon which it was founded by
Christ. The church has failed because it has ceased to maintain the unity of the Spirit, and consequently the unity of
the body.[9]

In the so-called church of today, ministry has become a
worldly ordinance in which a clergyman is a minister irrespective of any grace or gift, and thus the nominal authority of
God's office is attached to every error, unbelief, and evil within the church. The Spirit of God has been totally rejected as

3. J. N. Darby, *Churches and the Church,* Col. Writ., Eccl. Vol. IV,
p. 487.

4. J. N. Darby, *On the Presence and Action of the Holy Spirit in the
Church,* Col. Writ., Eccl. Vol. I, p. 417.

5. J. N. Darby, *What Is the Church,* Col. Writ., Eccl. Vol. III, p. 127.

6. J. N. Darby *Review of a Sermon,* Col. Writ., Eccl. Vol. III, p. 399.

7. J. N. Darby, *A Glance at Various Ecclesiastical Principles,* Col.
Writ., Eccl. Vol. II, p. 16.

8. J. N. Darby, *The Nature and Unity of the Church of Christ,* Col.
Writ., Eccl. Vol. I, p. 33.

9. J. N. Darby, *What Is the Unity of the Church,* Col. Writ., Eccl.
Vol. IV, p. 459.

the guide of worship, so that the worshipper has no sure contact with God.   Indiscriminate communion of believers and unbelievers proclaims the positive compatibility of unholiness and Christian privilege, becoming automatic by canon law and ecclesiastical practice — the sanction for ungodliness in the church, the nursery of apostasy in the midst of believers.   Unsoundness of doctrine insures an improper balance of spiritual growth; the association of forgiveness and regeneration with the visible signs of admission — baptism and the sacraments — precludes the purity of "believers only" in the church.   Its members meet as members of a parish, not as members of Christ.[10]

> . . . Satan having beguiled the Church, the church is in the position
> of earthliness and united in system with the world: he has got it
> while it was in its low state, tied down by its own will first, then
> by actual bonds into the unhallowed union which makes it a bar,
> and a hindrance to the Spirit of God . . . .[11]

This ruin in which the church finds itself is not merely one of denominational division; *it is one in which the entire nature and purpose of the church has become so perverted that it is diametrically opposed to the fundamental reason for which it was instituted.*[12]

The cause of this corruption is man's failure to apprehend fully his relation to Christ: a relation of obedience and glory. Man has sought his own way instead of the glory of Christ: he has attempted to erect a system instead of keeping the deposit of truth that was entrusted to him.[13]

> This has led to division and disunity. The church is filled with con-
> flicting ideologies and principles which dissipate the glory of Christ.
> The church — once beautiful, united, heavenly — has lost its char-
> acter, is hidden in the world; and the Christians themselves are
> worldly, covetous, eager for riches, honor, power — like the children
> of the ages.[14]

Hence the church, as the visible form of Christ's body, has lost its original state; it no longer exhibits the *visible unity* where

---

10. J. N. Darby, *Reply to a Tract, Entitled, "Our Separating Brethren,"*
Col. Writ., Eccl. Vol. III, p. 225, *passim.*

11. *Ibid.,* p. 222.

12. Darby, *What Is the Unity of the Church,* p. 456.

13. Darby, *On the Formation of Churches,* p. 314.

14. Darby, *What Is the Church,* p. 130.

the Holy Spirit displays His power so that the grace of Christ might be manifest in it.

It is not merely that the church has become corrupted, and has lost its effectiveness. *The church is in ruins!* It has become a corrupt mass, an apostasy hastening to its final consummation, rather than the symbol of a dispensation which God is sustaining through His faithful grace.[15] The Holy Spirit is not owned as its power; unity in the sense of a visible body on earth is lost; the sense of responsibility to be *one* as a testimony on the earth has been erased; its spiritual character has been replaced; its principle of action as to the workings of the Spirit has been laid aside and replaced by a human system, which does not recognize the action of the members of the body.[16]

> I fully recognize that there was an organization in apostolic and scriptural times, but affirm that what now exists is not the scriptural organization at all, but mere human invention, each sect arranging itself according to its own convenience, so that as an external body, the Church is ruined; and though much may be enjoyed of what belongs to the Church, I believe from Scripture that the ruin is without remedy, that the professing church will be cut off.[17]

Darby regards the church as a dispensation which, like all other dispensations, has failed and must suffer the judgment of God. As Adam fell; as Noah sinned after building an altar of thanksgiving; as the Israelites made a golden calf immediately after God spoke to them out of the midst of fire; as the sons of Aaron offered strange fire; as the son of David turned to idolatry and the kingdom was ruined; man corrupted the church.[18] As Israel has been cut off, so will the church; and as a remnant will be saved out of Israel, so there is hope that a remnant of the church may be used to glorify Christ.[19]

15. J. N. Darby, *The Apostasy of the Successive Dispensations,* Col. Writ., Eccl. Vol. I, p. 190.

16. J. N. Darby, *Thoughts on the Church,* Col. Writ., Eccl. Vol. IV, p. 523.

17. J. N. Darby, *What the Christian Has Amid the Ruins of the Church,* Col. Writ., Eccl. III, p. 417.

18. J. N. Darby, *The Church — the House and the Body,* Col. Writ., Eccl. Vol. III, p. 151.

19. J. N. Darby, *Remarks on the State of the Church,* Col. Writ., Eccl. Vol. I, p. 362.

This corruption of the church has been predicted from the beginning: in fact, the church began to be corrupted soon after its inception. "The failure of the outward professing church is a positive declaration of Scripture . . . that perilous times would come in the last days.[20]   John states there were anti-christs in his day; Peter declares that the time has come for judgment to begin at the house of the Lord; and Paul found evil men and seducers already creeping in. Corruption of the purity and unity of the church began in its early days, and it has been continuously in a decline until now it is in ruins.

> The first Epistle of John shows the church in ruins . . . that it was *in* the church that the anti-Christ was to arise, and, that this evil already existed in the days of the apostles. It was indeed the last time, for this moral character, this essential character, was already there. The Church ought to have been the perfect testimony of what Christ is; whereas it had become the cradle of corruption — the formal denial of Christ . . . .[21]

That the church is responsible for its present state of corruption and ruin is beyond question.   Its entire history has been a deviation from its true principles.   It has become consumed with "making a system"; with seeking human leadership; with desire for numbers instead of genuine converts; with human righteousness, ordinances, succession, ceremonial observances, professional ministry, carnal procedures — confusing spiritual administration with human imagination.

It has not been faithful to the command of Christ to glorify Him; has not sought the wisdom and guidance of the Holy Spirit; has not committed itself to the task of obedient service in His kingdom, but rather, has contented itself with the luxuries of a vast and complex system of orders instead of freedom in the Spirit; pastoral supervision instead of the priesthood of all believers; governing bodies and boards instead of the presidency of the Holy Spirit; ritual instead of simple and direct exercise of the soul toward God; ecclesiastical ethics instead of obedience to God's command; pomp and pretense instead of humbleness of soul; and derived authority instead of the gift of God to minister.[22]   It has given itself to an adula-

20. J. N. Darby, *Discipline and Unity in the Church*, Col. Writ., Eccl. Vol. IV, p. 396.

21. Darby, *Thoughts on the Church*, p. 525.

22. J. N. Darby, *The Character of Office in the Present Dispensation*, Col. Writ., Eccl. Vol. I, p. 169.

tion of everything which supports the interest of class and party, at the expense of faith, the action of the Spirit, the Word, and truth.

What then is the future of the church? As a dispensation it has failed; it has lost its place in God's economy; it will be judged on that account, although the faithful within the church are sure of being saved.

> We insist on the fact that the house has been ruined, its ordinances perverted, its orders and all its arrangements forsaken or destroyed; that human ordinances, a human order, have been substituted for them; and, what merits all attention of faith, we insist that the Lord . . . is coming soon in His power and glory to judge all this state of things.[23]

As God has cut off other dispensations, so will He do with the church. Because of its iniquity and apostasy, God cut off Israel as regards the covenant, but took out of it a remnant, which became the church. In the same way, "what concerns the church on earth, the house of God through the Spirit, it will exist no more."[24] However, "Christ has attached its practical operations to two or three, and owns them by His presence. He has provided for its maintenance. Thus, in all states of ruin it cannot cease, till He ceases to be the Head, and the Holy Spirit to be as the Guide and Comforter sent down."[25] Failure though there may be, the church still is His dwelling-place, and will ever be. The remnant to be taken from the church in ruins is to be the Assembly.[26]

The believer has a responsibility to this church in ruins, but not to restore it. Any attempt to restore the church will result in utter failure, since it is neither in God's will that the church be restored, nor does man have the authority to do so: he is utterly incapable.[27] All efforts to repair the ruins are not only sinful, but quite beyond the strength of the churches.[28] God has never restored a fallen dispensation to its original state, but has always proceeded to a new medium of deal-

23. Darby, *A Glance . . . at Principles*, p. 16.
24. Darby, *What Is the Church*, p. 130.
25. J. N. Darby, *Two Letters as to Plymouth*, Col. Writ., Eccl. Vol. IV, p. 29.
26. By the Assembly, Darby means his own group, the Brethren.
27. Darby, *On the Formation of Churches*, p. 217.
28. Darby, *What Is the Unity of the Church*, p. 455.

ing with man. Man cannot begin the church again, for God
is not beginning it.

> [Scripture does not] present the restoration of a dispensation; it
> never justifies its actual condition; though grace may . . . effect
> revivals during the longsuffering of God, the dispensation, as such,
> is actually gone, that the glory of the principle contained in it
> may shine forth in the hands of the Messiah. The attempt to set
> this dispensation on another footing, as to its continuance . . .
> shows ignorance of the principles of God's dealing . . . .[29]

"Obedience to God, and not imitation of the apostle" is
the duty of the believer as he views this ruined and condemned
church.[30]   God has given the believer instructions: "from such
turn away" (II Tim. 3:5) ; "be not unequally yoked together
with unbelievers" (II Cor. 6:14) ; "purge the vessels of dishonor" (I Cor. 6:9) ; and "depart from iniquity" (II Tim.
2:19) .

> Two great principles remain for the sincere Christian. It is posi-
> tively stated (2 Tim. iii) that the church would fail and become
> as bad as heathenism; and the Christian is directed to turn away
> from evil and turn to the scriptures, and Christ (Rev. ii and iii)
> is revealed as judging the state of the churches, and the individual
> is called to listen to what He says as to judging the churches; so
> that the church cannot have authority over the Christian, for he
> is to listen to Christ judging it.[31]

Believers are to forsake the government and order of man
which has corrupted the church, and assemble in simple unity.
"Our business is not to originate a church of the present or
future, but to cleanse the church God has made, and consequently to confess the sin of all rivals, to repudiate them, and
to come out from them.[32] The only true course for believers
is to withdraw from all religious societies called "churches"
and to meet "in the name of the Lord Jesus" — to call together
the true assembly of God.

> He has told us when the church was become utterly corrupt, as
> He declared it would, we were to turn away from all this cor-
> ruption and those who were in it, and turn to the scriptures which
> "are able to make the man of God wise unto salvation."[33]

29. Darby, *The Apostasy of Successive Dispensations,* p. 197.
30. *Loc. cit.*
31. Darby, *God, Not the Church,* p. 379.
32. J. N. Darby, *Lectures on the Church of God,* Col. Writ., Eccl.
Vol. III, p. 37.
33. Darby, *God, Not the Church,* p. 366.

Separation is not enough: it has in it no uniting power. Some positive principle is needed to secure the cohesion of those who have withdrawn from the corruption. This can be found only in Christ, who is the true center of unity, and who through His mediatorial powers can unite the assembly of God as its redeemer, its head, and its life.

This assembly must have the power of the Holy Spirit in order to gather the believers who forsake the corruption of an apostate church. Believers do not need to wait until that power produces an organized union, for "two or three gathered in my name" may act in reliance upon the promise of blessing given by God. The assembly is to be a single gathering of all believers, without pomp or ritual, with strict adherence to the Scriptures for all procedure, and with reliance upon the Holy Spirit as the source of its power.

The responsibility for this assembly lies with the Brethren.

> The presence of the Holy Ghost in the Church as one body was the grand doctrine on which the whole testimony of the Brethren was founded . . . *the testimony was especially committed to the Brethren.*[34]

Darby rejects with utter disregard all claims of others to be the true representatives of Christ's body on earth, and makes for the Brethren a sole claim to this distinction. Only the Brethren gather in His name. Others gather as Baptist, Congregationalist, etc., not as "His body." Only the Assembly (Brethren) is the church of God on earth.

> I cannot think any, even the most zealous of those persons who, with a desire of which I willingly acknowledge the sincerity, have sought to again set up the fallen dispensation . . . are in a condition to be able to do it, or that they have the right to impose upon my faith, as God's church, the little edifices they have set up . . . . I know that those who esteem these little organized societies to be the church of God, see nothing but mere meetings of men in every other gathering of God's children. There is a very simple answer on this matter. Such brethren have no promise authorizing them to again set up the churches of God when they

---

34. J. N. Darby, *A Letter to the Saints in London, As to the Presence of the Holy Ghost in the Church,* Col. Writ., Eccl. III, pp. 5, 6.

have fallen, whilst there is positive promise that where two or three are gathered together in the name of Jesus He is in the midst.[35]

Within the principles briefly summarized above, Darby consigns the entire professing church in visible form to the judgment of a dispensation of failure and enumerates the principle of believer-assembly which has characterized the Brethren movement. Precisely the same beliefs about apostate Christendom and separate assembly are held by contemporary dispensationalists.

The Nature of the Church

Though the visible manifestation of the church is in ruins, Christ's body, as the actual church, cannot be marred: it is what Christ is building for final presentation to Himself. The ambiguity of the word "church" leads to confusion, as Darby noted:

> What does it mean? Mr. G's congregation might build him a new church: then it means a building. Or, Mr. S. may be a member of Mr. G's church; then it means an assembly under the presidency of Mr. G. In England, he is going into the church means he is going to become a clergyman; he is going to church, is the public service of worship — gone to church is the building again.[36]

It is more correct to think of the body of Christ as the "assembly" rather than as the "church," since the word *ecclesia*

35. J. N. Darby, *Reflections on the Ruined Conditions of the Church*, Col. Writ., Eccl. Vol. III, pp. 11, 24. It does not concern Darby that there has been no evidence of this assembly from Pentecost until its truth was given to the Brethren. "It matters little to us if ecclesiastical historians have failed in their interesting researches to discern a single trace of the true expression of God's assembly from the close of the Apostolic era to the beginning of the present century. It is quite possible that there may have been here and there amid the thick gloom of the Middle Ages, 'two or three' really gathered in the Name of Jesus, or at least those who sighed after the truth of such a thing. But, be this as it may, it leaves that truth wholly untouched . . . . Although it could be proved that for eighteen hundred years there were not even two or three gathered in the name of Jesus, that would not in the smallest degree affect the question. The word is not 'What saith the ecclesiastical historian?' but, 'What saith the Scriptures?" C. H. Mackintosh, *The Assembly of God, or, The All-Sufficiency of the Name of Jesus*. London: G. Morrish, n.d., p. 43. While this statement does not come directly from Darby, it reflects his attitude as expressed repeatedly in many of his writings.

36. J. N. Darby, *Church and Privileges*, Col. Writ., Eccl. Vol. IX, p. 426.

is more accurately translated "assembly." In his own version of the New Testament, Darby invariably translated *ecclesia* as *assembly.* "The assemblies . . . being edified" (Acts 9:31) ; "Take heed . . . to shepherd the assemblies" (Acts 20:28) ; and "All assemblies of Christ salute you" (Rom. 16:16) .

The assembly, in Darby's sense, is more than just the gathering of Christians: it is the gathering of believers "in His name." Believers do not gather "in His name" merely by professing to do so, but only as they conform to the ideal which Christ has established. Baptists, for example, cannot invoke His blessings, however sincere they may be, by merely meeting as Christians, for they are still within the ruins of a professing church.

The assembly is constituted by believers *who have gathered in the Lord's name*:

> . . . supposing ten thousand Christians, meeting simply as Christians, is that enough? I can conceive an assembly of professing, yea, real Christians: yet there would be no reason to call them God's assembly. *It is not the fact of being a Christian that constitutes God's assembly, but their being gathered in the name of the Lord.*[37]

To be gathered in His name means to conform to the provisions which He has established, namely, to allow the free rule of the Spirit in building up the body of Christ without external authority or organized societies — all of which hinder the Spirit. Other Christian groups could so meet, except that they are committed to the extraneous organization of the professing church. It is not that the Brethren have an exclusive possession of truth, but simply that one cannot meet "in His name," as here defined, if he meets in a professing church that denies the provisions of "His name."

This decidedly restricts the scope of the church. Darby narrows the fellowship of the church to include only those who meet according to his principles. His controversies repeatedly demonstrated that anyone who did not agree with his definition of the church was immediately consigned to apostasy. How tragically similar this attitude is to the conclusion that anyone not adhering to dispensational truth is not "rightly dividing the Word of God."

37. Darby, *Lectures on the Church of God*, p. 256.

Historical Genesis of the Church

The church (i.e., the true church or assembly) did not come into existence until Pentecost, at which time Christ, through the Holy Spirit, took a remnant of Israel, to which believing Gentiles were added, and formed His assembly.[38] It began "or was found existing, at the soonest when Christ was glorified in the heavens . . . . the church [was] formed on earth by the Holy Ghost . . . after the glorification of Christ."[39]

> There never was a Jewish church. The church, even in its outward profession, stands by faith — is never composed of natural branches. The Jews were natural branches. They did not, in their divinely-ordained place as Jews, stand by faith. A Jewish church is an unscriptural fallacy.[40] . . . The church is composed, according to Scripture, only of the saints from Pentecost till the Lord comes to receive it to himself.[41]

The Abrahamic covenant was to Israel alone; it contained local blessings and promises to Israel, but contained no promise of the church, and did not reach beyond the original promises to the families on earth.[42] "The body of the church could not exist before the glorification of Jesus, for this would have been a body without a Head. . . ."[43]

> What gave rise to the existence of the so-called Plymouth Brethren is the grand truth, the great fact, of the descent of the Holy Ghost *on the day of Pentecost* to form the body of Christ in one . . . .[44]

While the church was not revealed in the Old Testament the assembly was, for Israel was the assembly of God by birth: God dwelt among them as His people. When Israel rejected Christ, however, God judged them, sparing only a remnant through which Israel's glory could later be re-established (Isaiah 8).

The assembly formed through this remnant did not constitute a continuation of the covenant with Israel. Rather, there

---

38. Darby, *God, Not the Church*, p. 366.
39. Darby, *What Is the Church*, pp. 116-117.
40. J. N. Darby, *Law*, Col. Writ., Eccl. Vol. III, p. 15.
41. J. N. Darby, *Brethren and Their Reviewers*, Col. Writ., Eccl. Vol. III, p. 71.
42. J. N. Darby, *The Covenants*, Col. Writ., Eccl. Vol. IV, p. 13. The reader will note that this is a different tract from the one of the same name, noted in footnote 33, page 26 from Col. Writ., Doc. Vol. I.
43. Darby, *Thoughts on the Church*, p. 514.
44. Darby, *What Is the Unity of the Church*, p. 453.

was an abrupt change. The assembly was set on redemption-grounds, gathered to Christ as His body on earth; it was founded on the atonement of Christ and the power of His resurrection. Because this redemption-ground brought Christ personally into their midst through the baptism of the Holy Ghost, their gathering was a true place of meeting where the Lord was. The assembly thus became the body of Christ and a habitation of God. Christ owned it formally as His assembly on the earth. The title "church" (assembly) became the generic name for the assembly of God among men.[45]

The assembly (church) may be regarded in two aspects: as the body of Christ, and as the habitation of God.

The Church as the Body of Christ

As the body of Christ, the assembly is more than just the group of "called-out" believers: it is the actual embodiment of Christ in the world.[46] It is Christ living in the believers to bring into being His testimony on the earth. He works in the soul of the believer — a real, spiritual work, applicable individually and only to those who, through His grace, have been baptized into Him by the Holy Spirit. "The true body of Christ . . . is composed of those who are united to Christ by the Holy Ghost, who, when the professing church is cut off will have their place with him in heaven. . . ."[47]

The expression "the body of Christ" is not merely a metaphor to express certain characteristics of the church, though certain metaphors do exist in the Scriptures. The church *is* the body of Christ in a very literal sense. It is a living organism, pulsating with a vibrant expression of its vitality, and extending itself into the organic life of its members. It draws its sustenance from Christ, who necessarily nourishes and cherishes it as His own flesh, as members of His own body.[48]

This union with Christ is precisely that which makes the church distinctively post-Pentecostal. The Old Testament saints had possessed life through faith, but they could not be identified in union with Christ at the right hand of God, since

45. J. N. Darby, *The House of God, the Body of Christ, and the Baptism of the Holy Ghost,* Col. Writ., Eccl. Vol. III, pp. 27-30.
46. Darby, *Churches and the Church,* p. 480.
47. Darby, *What the Christian Has Amid the Ruins,* p. 417.
48. Darby, *Two Letters as to Plymouth,* p. 289.

He had not yet established their redemption. They had
a faith that looked to the future; their relationship with God
was one of covenant and law. On the cross, Christ entered into
the judgment, bore the wrath of God, and by His death provided the means whereby believers might be established in a
new relationship — redemption.[49] He was *the* redemption,
and in presenting redeemed believers, He presented them unto
Himself. Believers were, therefore, identified with Him: they
became His body.

This identification constitutes a union, not in name only, but
in fact. The believer is wrought into Christ by the Holy Spirit
who dwells in him, making the body of the believer His temple
(I Cor. 6:19). He seals the believer until the day of redemption (Eph. 1:13, 4:30), and baptizes him with other
saints into one body — Christ (I Cor. 12:13). "Now ye are
the body of Christ, and members in particular. . . . For as the
body is one and hath many members, and all the members of
that one body, being many, are one, so also is the Christ"
(I Cor. 12:27, 12).

Christ has "quickened the dead in trespasses and sin," and
God has "raised us up together, and made us sit in heavenly
places in Christ Jesus" — not simply with, but *in* Jesus. Just
as Christ occupies a position of glory in the sight of the
Father, the believer occupies the same position *in Christ*. He
thus is not merely identified with Christ, *he is the body of
Christ.*[50]

The body of Christ, moreover, is more than just the sum
total of believers on earth. While it contains all believers, *it
does not exist merely because there is a body of believers, but it
is a separate entity into which believers are brought* — a spiritual union accomplished by the Holy Spirit who *creates* the
believer in Christ, hence as a part of His body.[51] This union
is a heavenly existence. The church is not earthly, but heavenly, since its existence is in Christ. The church would exist
even if there were no believers, since the church is in Christ,
and believers are baptized into a relation to Christ. This concept has important implications for Darby's eschatology: it
is one of the bases for the rapture — since it is heavenly in

49. Darby, *The House . . . the Body . . . the Baptism,* p. 36.
50. J. N. Darby, *The Church, an Habitation of God Through the
Spirit,* Col. Writ., Evan. Vol. I, p. 371.
51. Darby, *The House . . . the Body . . . the Baptism,* p. 49.

character, the church must be raptured out of the earthly tribulation. Only Israel has an earthly existence.

The expression of Christ's body on the earth is the assembly, and in this sense the assembly is said to be the body of Christ. The various members of the body are wrought in the Holy Spirit to perform various functions, and God is said to have set them in the assembly. Thus the assembly is called the body, and the members are set in the assembly, so that the assembly is said to be the body of Christ.[52]

Darby does not refer to the assembly as a formal organization. Neither a body of professors nor an external corporation can occupy a relation of identity to Christ. Between Christ and the church as a society there is no organic connection such as exists between the members of a human body and the head, or between the branches of a tree and the tree itself. *Only individual believers are in Christ,* as the branch is in the vine.

There is, in reality, no such thing as Christ dwelling in the church, if the church be viewed as something distinct from the individuals which compose it. If societies may be said to have Christ as their head, it is not by direct union, but mediately; that is, it is because the individuals of which they are composed are in union with Him. The societies may be churches of Christ, but it is the individuals who compose them who are members of Christ's body. Only as the assembly is viewed as identical with the actual union of believers can it be said to be the body of Christ.

Even though the term "body of Christ" is not to be regarded as a metaphor, its functions can be likened to that of a human body with its various members performing individual functions, each contributing to the function of the whole. God has placed various functions within the church, each distinctively different from the other. In the exercise of these functions, unity, diversity, and mutual interdependence of each other contribute to the total function of the body, so that the total witness of the assembly is made known.

The Church as the Habitation of God

Just as it is the body of Christ, the assembly is the habitation of God on earth. Again, this expression is no mere metaphor:

52. Darby, *The House . . . the Body . . . the Baptism,* p. 49.

God actually lives in the world through His habitation in the assembly.

This habitation of God constitutes a new relationship between God and man. He did not dwell with Adam or Abraham, but merely "visited them."[53]   As soon as Israel was redeemed out of Egypt, and the tabernacle built, God said, "I will *dwell* in the midst of Israel, and I will be their God" (Exod. 29:45) .   The redemption out of Egypt was specifically for the purpose that God might "dwell with them."   After the tabernacle, God dwelt in the temple.   When Christ came to earth, He dwelt in Him.   Now that believers, through identification with His death and sacrifice, become a part of Christ's body, God dwells with them through the Holy Spirit.   Since believers comprise the assembly, God is viewed as dwelling in the assembly.   Thus the tabernacle of God (the assembly) is with man on earth.

However, like the body of Christ, the habitation is not something that automatically grows out of a meeting of believers: it is that which God has created to which believers may be added.

> His own grace has built a habitation for himself . . . . [This is] not a place of glory into which we are to come before God, but . . . God will come down and dwell here upon the earth When Jesus was in the world, God's presence was there . . . . now, it is the same thing with regard to the church, as a "habitation," though not visibly, not in manifested glory.[54]

As a habitation, the church is viewed as formed on earth; Jews and Gentiles alike are builded together for a habitation of God through the Spirit.   "Here the divine point was God in the Spirit dwelling in a house.   He is himself joined to nobody.   It is a mere dwelling-place which is formed, and in which He is found . . . . the principle on which it is formed . . . [is] Jesus himself being the corner stone."[55]   It is "those who are His redeemed ones, brought together by the peace which Christ preaches, who have, through Christ, access by one Spirit, that comes to be the place where God dwells.[56]

53. J. N. Darby, *Reply to Judge Marshall's Tract On the Tenets of the Plymouth Brethren (so called)*, Col. Writ., Doc. Vol. IX, p. 527.

54. Darby, *The Church, an Habitation* . . ., p. 365.

55. J. N. Darby, *Ephesians*, Col. Writ., Eccl. Vol. IV, p. 498.

56. Darby, *The Church, an Habitation* . . . , p. 372.

As with the body, the basis of God's habitation among men is the redemption wrought by Christ. "The dwelling of God with man is the fruit of redemption."[57] Christ, having wrought this redemption, having ascended to God and seated on His right hand, having quickened us to life, and having gathered us together, makes us, thus gathered,

> . . . an habitation of God through the Spirit. It is not God merely acting in certain men; it is God dwelling in the church down here, as gathered through the word of the gospel. The church is the place of God's presence on the earth. He has set us in redemption, and comes and dwells in us. When the church was gathered together in one accord in one place, at Pentecost, the Holy Ghost came down and dwelt there, the result of the accomplished work of Jesus . . . . [This] is the presence of God Himself.[58]

It is upon the ground of God's perfect and entire complacency in the church, thus wrought by the redemption of Christ, that He comes to dwell in it. He does not come to test man's faith and obedience, as He did with Abraham or with Israel, but comes to delight in a faith completed by Christ.

> He says, as it were, "I have so accomplished this redemption, I am so pleased with you, so satisfied because of Jesus, that I am come to dwell with you, to make my abode with you: you are my habitation."[59]

As the habitation of God, the church does not dwell *with* God, but becomes the dwelling place *of* God.

> . . . God has formed a habitation for Himself where He dwells by His Spirit. It is so indeed as to the individual (1 Cor. vi), but now I speak of the assembly, the house of the living God. *This is now on earth, the habitation of God by His Spirit.*[60]

The "habitation" is also viewed as *God's building* (I Cor. 3:9); as an edifice already in existence in which God is now dwelling, and also as a building under construction — a process of being edified.[61] The word used in I Corinthians 3:9 is translated in I Corinthians 14:3 in the sense of edification, or being built up in a spiritual way. As a completed building, the assembly exists for God's testimony on earth; in the

57. Darby, *Churches and the Church,* p. 481.
58. Darby, *The Church, an Habitation* . . . , p. 372.
59. *Ibid.,* p. 375.
60. Darby, *Churches and the Church,* p. 481. Italics added.
61. J. N. Darby, *The Gospel and the Church according to the Scripture,* Col. Writ., Eccl. Vol. VIII, p. 534.

process of edification it looks to the day in which it will be completed as the *true tabernacle* of God, a spiritual house including all believers. As the completed building, the assembly is viewed as the work of Christ: He builds, and no other instrumentality is used. As the house being built, however, it has been entrusted to the responsibility of man who has implicit instructions on how to govern the church.

In Ephesians 2:21, the habitation is regarded as the temple of God, "In whom all the building fitly framed together groweth unto a holy temple in the Lord: for an habitation of God through the Spirit." The holy temple embraces the whole church from Pentecost to the coming of the Lord. In the expression "temple of the Lord," the thought of God's dwelling in the church is reiterated.

Christ, the Head of the Church

A careful analysis of the Scriptures relating to the church reveals that it is always subordinate and subservient to Christ: He is the head of the church. This establishes a relationship in which the vital energy animating the whole church flows directly from, and by virtue of, a real incorporation of Christ in His church.

Christ is head not only of the church: He is head of *all* principality and power (Col. 1:18), of creation and all things that exist (Eph. 1:22). His relation to the church suggests that it has a place in the eternal purposes of God in the final subjection of all things to Christ. The church occupies a unique position in God's plan, for, while Christ is head of all things by creation, He is head of the church by redemption.

This unique position places the church in the forefront of Christ's interest. It is His church; bought by His sacrifical death; redeemed by His atoning blood; founded on faith given by and in Him; kept by the power of His word; sustained and energized by His Comforter; established in heavenly places by His glory; and to be presented to the Father through His holiness. It is His bride, His virgin, His body, His life, His flock. He is its guide, its shepherd, its way, its life, its truth. It exists in Him, for Him, and to Him. In being established by Him, it proceeds from Him, that it may return to Him.

The church, consequently, is to share His glory.[62] While

62. Darby, *The Gospel and Church* . . . , p. 533.

all things will be put under His feet, the church will reign with Him as joint-heirs of all the inheritance of heaven. Thus the church is the *ultimate* of God's plan for man. All other dispensations were conditional, with the responsibility resting on man; but the church is not conditioned, because Christ has sole responsibility for its existence, and for its future.

The Church on Earth

Darby's view of the church on earth must be understood in juxtaposition with his doctrine of the "heavenly" church. Ideally, the church is a heavenly entity composed of "heavenly people" who are to be associated with Him in His glory — a system forming no part of this earthly system. As Christ's church, they belong to heaven; their place in the restitution of all things is *there*. They are formed into a spiritual community; delivered in spirit out of this present world, becoming spiritual in their interest, thoughts, and prospects. "The *purposes* of God for the assembly have their aim in heaven . . . [while] the *ways* of God are accomplished and unfolded on the earth for our instructions, both in the assembly and in individuals."[63]

Yet the church, this heavenly body, exists in title only; it has not yet been formed. It has a "mystic perfection in the mind of God,"[64] but exists as to fact only in its earthly form. What is viewed as the church on earth is the formation of that body, which is to be completed, and heavenly, when Christ shall gather it for Himself. "Until He rises up [sic] from His seat on high, He is working and ordering and acting always (while hid in God) by the Holy Ghost: and the Holy Ghost is down here. That which he owns as the Church is where the Holy Ghost is, until it is united to Himself in glory."[65]

> The body, if any place be spoken of, is always spoken of as on the earth . . . . The body is formed by the baptism of the Holy Ghost sent down from heaven, and of course, formed on the earth: and *though I doubt not that that which is the body be in heaven,*

63. J. N. Darby, *Synopsis of the Bible*. London: G, Morrish, n.d., third edition, revised, IV, 280.

64. J. N. Darby, *Notes on the Revelation*, Col. Writ., Pro. Vol. I, p. 263.

65. J. N. Darby, *The Church — What Is It? Her Power, Hopes, Calling, Present Position and Occupation*, Col. Writ., Evan. Vol. I, p. 568.

> *the body and heaven are never connected together,* because it is
> formed by the Holy Spirit come down from heaven.[66]

As both the body of Christ and the habitation of God, the
church is viewed as earthly: it is the place of God on the earth.
Christ's declaration of His intention to build the church "on
this rock" proves the church to have an earthly character. In
Acts we read that the Lord "added to the church daily," which
is an earthly adding. When Paul refers to "them within and
them that are without" in I Corinthians 5:12 he refers "clearly
not within or without a particular assembly . . . [it] applies
to *the whole assembly of Christ on earth* . . . ."[67]

> In 1 Corinthians 5:12 'one body, many members' . . . . shows that
> the local assembly, viewed in association with all Christians every-
> where on the earth, particularly represents and acts for all saints
> with the Lord's authority if gathered in His name, yet it shows
> that the apostle has in mind THE assembly, not *an* assembly.[68]

Whenever there is a reference to a gift of ministry, it is always
with a localized setting: gifts are given to the church, earthly
gifts of activity and energy which can be exercised only in an
earthly church.

The church on earth is visible: it is not merely visible
churches, but *a* visible church. The visibility of the body
"connects itself with . . . the presence and action of the Holy
Ghost on earth. It is not merely a saved thing in the counsel
of God, but a living thing animated down here by its union with
the Head, and the presence of the Holy Ghost in it.[69]

The purpose of the earthly existence of the church is the
manifestation of the activity of God's love and holiness through
the power of the Holy Spirit.[70] For this reason it was gathered
as a remnant from Israel, and when this testimony has been
completed it will be given its heavenly character in the glory of
Christ. Until that time the church labors through its gifts
"for the perfecting of the saints . . . unto the *building up* of
the Body of Christ."[71] The body is not yet complete, nor will

66. J. N. Darby, *The Church, Which is His Body: a Letter on A. R. D.'s
Few Thoughts as to the Position of the Saints Gathered in the Name of
the Lord*, Eccl. Vol. IV, p. 324. Italics added.
67. Darby, *Discipline and Unity in the Church*, p. 397.
68. *Ibid.*, p. 398.
69. Darby, *Two Letters as to Plymouth*, p. 291.
70. Darby, *Thoughts on the Church*, p. 513.
71. Eph. 4:12.

it be until the work of the church has been consummated in Christ.

This incompleteness of the body of Christ is the explanation of the earthly existence of the church. The church is not constituted by the multiple gathering of all believers, but by every individual gathering of believers in His name. Scripture does not speak of the church of Galatia, but of the churches of Galatia: conversely, it refers to the church at Ephesus, but never to the churches of Ephesus. The expression "church of God" applies to a company of believers gathered in His name in the locality *in which they reside*. Hence there can be no universal church in the literal earthly sense. Each assembly is an autonomous local congregation with its own administrative privileges.[72] It answers only to the rule of the Holy Spirit.

Every church meeting in Christ's name within a geographical area constitutes the assembly of God in that area.[73]

> Observe that, although the assembly at Corinth was only a part of that body of Christ, the apostle speaks of the whole body; for the assembly there was, according to the principles of its gathering, the body of Christ as asembled at Corinth . . . . the Christians of one town were considered as representing the whole assembly, as far as regards that locality.[74]

There is, therefore, no such thing in Scripture as a central authority having jurisdictional control over a group of churches. Each assembly is independently responsible to the Holy Spirit for the exercise of gifts under its own administration. It is not bound to other assemblies in a union of bylaws and creedal formulas, but in a fellowship of unity which is based on a mutual obedience to the Word, coming through the guidance of the Holy Spirit.

Each assembly, however, is independent in government only, not in existence as the sole body of Christ, for each assembly comprises the body of Christ.

72. Darby, *Synopsis of the Bible*, IV, 286.
73. Only those who meet according to the provisions established by God for His church actually meet "in His name." "While fully admitting that all Christians in a locality properly constitute the one assembly, if they will not unite, the responsibility and presence of the Lord are found with those who do, and their acts, if really done as met in His name, have His authority . . ." Darby, *Discipline and Unity in the Church*, p. 387.
74. Darby, *Synopsis of the Bible*, IV, 286-87.

> I do not admit, because scripture does not admit, independent as-
> semblies. There is the body of Christ, and all Christians are mem-
> bers of it, and the church of God in one place represents the whole
> and acts in its name.[75]
> There is one flock, and only one, meeting it may be in different
> localities, and elders belonging to these localities; but all the faith-
> ful there at any time were of it, because they were of God's flock.[76]

The individual assembly represents the whole assembly of
God. Individual believers in the assembly are members of
Christ, therefore of the whole body of Christ.

This doctrine gave Darby tremendous control over the
whole group. If a member was excluded by one assembly he
was forthwith declared to be outside the *entire* body of Christ.
The practical consequences of this doctrine were that it established the grounds of independency for the dispensational
separatist movement and gave warrant to autonomous action
by any church independent of the larger fellowship of the total
body of Christ.

The Unity of the Church

One of Darby's most consistent emphases is the oneness, the
unity, of the assembly, which is not merely the invisible unity
of the church in heaven. "The church is not just a visible
representation of the heavenly unity, but is the real unity itself."[77] This unity is of the whole body in Christ, of the church
as a whole. There is but one church, as there is but one Lord,
one faith, and one baptism, where all are brought together in
Christ's body. The substance and reality of this unity is the
divinely appointed plan of God to draw all believers into the
one body, and by so doing, to make His church united as one.

The presence of the Holy Spirit in the believer, and subsequently in the assembly, is the uniting factor that constitutes
the unity of the body. He has come down from heaven to
separate a peculiar people to Christ from the world, and,
through His gifts to the believers, effectively builds up of the
body of Christ is true unity.

75. J. N. Darby, *On Ecclesiastical Independency*, Col. Writ., Eccl. Vol. III,
p. 458.
76. Darby, *Review of a Sermon*, p. 388.
77. Darby, *Discipline and Unity in the Church*, p. 395.

> We cannot deny the body and its unity . . . and His operations in it, without denying the divine title of the Holy Ghost.[78]

> The Spirit is . . . the link between the assembly and Christ . . . . It is by the Spirit that communion is realized and maintained, it is the primary function of the Spirit . . . .[79]

Believers are baptized by the Spirit into the one body, hence, we are baptized into every other member of that body in a unity that makes the body one.

Only as the church is established in unity can it be the dwelling place of God. All believers, through the baptism of the Holy Spirit, are brought together in a oneness through which the assembly becomes both God's dwelling place and a testimony of His nature to the world. While the providence of God manifests His *power* in the works of creation and the government of the world, only through the Holy Spirit, and through Christ in the assembly, can His *presence* be manifested in the world.

The unity of the church, according to Darby, has a positive and a negative side. Positively, the church is one in Christ; negatively, it is one in its separation from evil. This unity is further analyzed in terms of three relationships: the church has unity *in Christ,* unity *within the assembly,* and unity *among assemblies.*

The basis of true unity, humanly speaking, is separation from all evil.[80] This evil manifests itself in two chief ways, ecclesiastical and personal. Ecclesiastical evil occurs when the church abandons the true principles instituted by God and becomes preoccupied with human organization. Personal evil occurs in the church because of the sins of its members. True unity cannot be achieved when these evils are present in the church.

The intrinsic power by which this unity is effected is Christ, for He alone is the true center of union. He is the object of divine counsel, the manifestation of God, the only vessel of mediatorial power, entitled to unite the assembly as its redeemer, its head, its glory, its life. Since the assembly exists as His body, He necessarily nourishes it with care and leader-

---

78. Darby, *Two Letters as to Plymouth,* p. 290.
79. Darby, *Synopsis of the Bible,* IV. 279.
80. J. N. Darby, *Separation From Evil, God's Principle of Unity,* Col. Writ., Eccl, Vol. I, p. 544.

ship. It is the depository of the glory of Christ, and is therefore the object of His desires. Establishing it on earth, and
building it into His completed body, He keeps it in the unity
of His own holiness, He is the one Lord over the church as
it is one body to Him.

This is not a unity produced by judicial power, but a
personal one. God is not yet separating the tares from the
wheat, but He has established Christ in the midst of the church
for cohesiveness through His personal holiness. Christ, therefore, becomes not only a center of unity of the universe by
creation, but He becomes a peculiar and special center of
divine affection in the assembly. This is no mere moral force
working within the assembly, but a personal manifestation of
the holiness of God by which His people are kept in Himself.

Just as the object around which the church coheres is Christ,
the character of the unity is heavenly, spiritual, otherworldly.
Yet the assembly is not to be taken out of the world, but kept
from evil and sanctified through the truth. Since the Holy
Spirit is the agent of this unity, He becomes its practical center.

> Its nature flows from God's; for of true unity He must be the
> centre, and He is holy; and He brings us into it by separating us
> from evil. Its object is Christ; He is sole centre of the church's
> unity, objectively as its Head. Its power is the presence of the Holy
> Spirit down here, sent as the spirit of truth withal from the Father
> by Jesus. Its measure is walking in the light, as God is in the
> light; fellowship with the Father, and with His Son Jesus, and we
> may add, through the testimony of the written word the apostolic
> and prophetic word especially.[81]

Unity within the assembly is the responsibility of believers,
and must be maintained by a strict avoidance of evil. Christ
cannot fail in His faithfulness to His body, but if the testimony
committed to the assembly is disrupted, it "is no longer
rendered as to make it felt that God is present on the earth."[82]

If the Spirit of God is denied the privilege of direct control,
the church is caused to deny the unity of the Body.[83] To appoint men who preside as sole teachers, to organize societies,
to impose creeds, to enforce external authority, is to usurp the

---

81. Darby, *Separation from Evil . . . Unity,* p. 555.
82. Darby, *Synopsis of the Bible,* IV, 279.
83. Darby, *Thoughts on the Church,* p. 513.

position of the Holy Spirit and to deny Him his rightful place in the assembly.

> Ecclesiastical authority, as such, as established by means of or-
> dinances, is always the enemy of truth. When . . . ministers lean
> upon authority, they are accredited as of God, but they do not
> allow God Himself to work outside those ordinances which give
> them their importance.[84]

Denominational forms of the church are in ruins because they fail to maintain the unity of the Spirit, and consequently the unity of the body. The responsibility of the believer in such a case is clear.

> Whenever the body declines putting away of evil, it becomes in
> its unity a denier of God's character of holiness, and the separation
> from evil is the path of the saint, and the unity he has left is the
> very greatest evil that can exist where the name of Christ is
> named.[85]

> The truth of Christ's gospel, or of godliness of walk, should never be
> sacrificed to outward unity.[86]

Unity among assemblies must be maintained through a mutual dependency upon the presidency of the Holy Spirit, and an allegiance to the Word. There is no such thing in Scripture as independent assemblies.

> The body of Christ on earth is composed of individuals and not
> churches. Now . . . there is unity only of the whole; there is none
> in the local assembly if it be detached from the whole. If it be
> regarded as an independent church, it has nothing to do with the
> body, it is not in principle an assembly of God.[87]

This unity, however, is not a communion among churches of all denominations, not an artificial combination of denom-inations, and not a unity of structure and constitution. It is a "true unity of the Spirit and it must be wrought by the operation of the Spirit."[88]

Outward union of Christian bodies produces confederacy,

84. J. N. Darby, *Notes on the Epistle to the Galatians*, London: G. Morrish, 1881, p. 8.

85. Darby, *Separation from Evil . . . Unity*, p. 15.

86. J. N. Darby, *The True Centre of Union*, Col. Writ., Doc. Vol. IV, p. 259.

87. Darby, *What Is the Unity of the Church*, p. 450.

88. J. N. Darby, *Scriptural Unity and Union*, Col. Writ., Doc. VIII, p. 489.

not unity, thus denying the nature of the church. Unity cannot be legislated or artifically formed; it must be the work of the Spirit, and can only be in the things of the Spirit, and therefore can only be perfected in spiritual persons. Man should not have to produce unity; yea, he cannot, for it is a state, not an act. Unity is absent only because worldly men attempt to gain authority and position in the church.

While man cannot produce unity in the church, he can place himself where the unity of the Spirit is not hindered: he can rely on the promise that where two or three are gathered in His name, the unity of the Spirit will be present.

The same responsibility exists between assemblies as with individuals. The instruction "ye are the body of Christ and members one of another," given to the Corinthian church, means that one assembly must receive a brother from another as being in the body of Christ.

Conversely, if one assembly judges an individual in discipline, for another assembly to receive him would be either to deny that the first assembly is a member of the body of Christ, or to deny the work of the Holy Spirit at that place. "Am I to then recognize [sic], as representing the unity of the body, and acting by the Spirit with the Lord's authority, an assembly which sanctions sin and says that it is not defiled by it?"[89] Assemblies must maintain the same vigilance to keep the unity of the body as must individuals.

The outward symbol of the unity of the assembly is the Lord's Table, for this is the act in which the dignity of the body of Christ is seen: ". . . it is the seal and symbol of the participation of all Christian privileges. We are identified with every person who partakes these, not only as to his being a child of God known to God, but as to his being one as known to us with all due spiritual investigation."[90]

The picture Darby paints of the relation of the individual believer to the Christ who makes the church is a recurring tendency in Protestant theology today, due to the emphasis placed on individual salvation.

89. Darby, *Discipline and Unity in the Church,* p. 385.
90. Darby, *Nature and Unity of the Church,* p. 38.

This views asserts that the church is not constituted by the gathering of believers, but they are added to the church — made to be a part of Christ's body. The question of the nature of the church is raised: Is there an entity already in existence called the church, into which the individual comes? This seems presupposed by Darby's insistence that it is Christ who makes the church what it is. Christ is there before the individual is redeemed, so that he enters into Christ, and hence, into Christ's body. Darby does not view the body of Christ as inoperative, but as being an entity into which the believer is brought, and in which he may have a relationship with Christ; the relationship itself does not constitute the body. The body is not formed by believers, but believers are made to be *in* the body, and to be part of the body. The church, therefore, could exist without the presence of a single believer, for Christ alone is the source and substance of His body, though it is naturally expressed in the earth in a visible form.

Darby is clearly at odds with most Protestant writers on the nature of the church. Few will agree with the idea that the church exists apart from the company of believers, maintaining that it is precisely the relation between Christ and the believers that constitutes the church. A suggestion of this is found in John Oman, who, evaluating the apostolic church, comments, "The church is . . . a unity of spirit through the one Spirit of God working in the individual members."[91]

He stands almost alone in asserting that the church is visible as to fact, and heavenly as to title. While not agreeing with the basic premise of Darby, and approaching the subject from a different standpoint, Bishop Gore refers to "the visible, actual church of which he [Paul] is speaking, the church to which Christ gave visible officers . . . ,"[92] as does Headlam: "It was a definite, concrete, visible body."[93] Hodge, on the other hand, asserts that it is not a visible body at all. "The church, as such is not a visible society. . . . It is not a corporation which

91. John Oman, *The Church and the Divine Order*. London: Hodder and Stoughton, 1911, p. 59.

92. Charles Gore, *The Ministry and the Christian Church*. London: Longmans, Green and Co., 1893, p. 48.

93. A. C. Headlam, *The Doctrine of the Church and Christian Reunion*. London: John Murray, 2nd edition, 1921, p. 198.

ceases to exist if the external bond of communion be dissolved."[94]

Heppe expresses the consensus of Protestant opinion, however, when he quotes Braun (II, iv, 24, 22, 7) as follows: "One and the same church may be called visible and invisible, but for a different reason. It is called visible, not only because men as men are visible, but because outwardly they profess Gospel truth and celebrate the sacraments according to the lawful use for which they were instituted by God. It ought to be called invisible because of the Spirit and true faith, which resides in the mind alone, which no man can see, which God alone knows."[95]   Beyschlag warns, however, as Darby most certainly would, that not all who "belong to the visible church are to be reckoned to the invisible, because they lack a living faith."[96]

While Darby treats the expression "body of Christ" as an actual entity that exists in Christ, most writers treat it as a "figure of speech" expressing a "metaphor," as T. G. Jallard terms it.[97]   E. Tyrell Green[98] calls it a "mystical union." Charles Hodge[99] calls it a "relation"; while it is described as an "image" by F. A. J. Hort.[100]

Darby will find few writers, outside of his own group of followers, who will admit the absolute distinction which he maintains between Israel and the church.   Hort says, "The Ecclesia of the ancient Israel was the Ecclesia of God; and now, having been confessed to be God's Messiah . . . He could to such hearers . . . claim that Ecclesia as His own.   What He declared that He would build was in one sense old, in another new.   It had a true continuity with the Ecclesias of the Old Covenant; the building of it would be a *re*building.   Christ's

94. Charles Hodge, *The Church and Its Policy*. London: Thomas Nelson and Sons, 1879, p. 5.

95. Heinrich Heppe. *Reformed Dogmatics*. London: George Allen and Unwin. Tr. G. T. Thompson, 1950, p. 668.

96. Willibald Beyschlag, *New Testament Theology*. Edinburgh: T & T. Clark. Tr. Neil Buchanan, 2nd edition, 1908, II, 231.

97. T. G. Jallard, *The Origin and Evolution of the Christian Church*. London: Hutchinson University Library, 1948, p. 59.

98. E. Tyrell Green, *The Church of Christ, Her Mission, Sacraments, and Discipline*. London: Methuen & Co., 902, p. 6.

99. *Ibid.*, p. 15.

100. F. A. J. Hort, *The Christian Ecclesia*. London: Macmillan & Co. Ltd., 1900, p. 16.

work in relation to it would be a completion of it, a bestowal on it of power to fulfill its yet unfulfilled Divine purposes. . . . Hence we go greatly astray if we interpret our Lord's use of the term *Ecclesia* in this cardinal passage [Matt. 16:18] exclusively by reference to the Ecclesia known to us in Christian history."[101]

Darby stands alone, other than among his immediate followers, on his assertion that the church is in ruins. Almost every scholar of repute would not only deny the charge, but vigorously contend that the church is militant, though at times showing evidence of the influence of worldliness, and is proceeding in the plan of God, earnestly awaiting the completion of His purposes in her.

It is appropriate to remark, in conclusion, that Darby's doctrine of the church is most important today for its practical effects, rather than for its theological arguments. If one believes that virtually all of Christendom is apostate, and that the unity of the church is maintained by separation from evil, then one will separate himself from that apostate Christendom. This is what the Darbyites did, and this is what the dispensationalists still do.

The separatist spirit and exclusivist attitude toward truth is one of the tragic aspects of the development of Darby's doctrine of the church. Is it too severe to say that the spirit of the movement is as important as its eschatological chronology? Is it too general a conclusion to say that the doctrines of dispensationalists have existed conjointly with the spirit of independency in church groups? Whatever evaluation history may make of this movement, it will attest that dispensationalism is rooted in Darby's concept of the church — a concept that sharply distinguishes the church from Israel, assigns an exclusivist role to the church in an apostate Christendom, gives the church a heavenly title and futuristic character, grants each local church independency because each comprises the body of Christ, and maintains unity through separation from evil.

101. *Ibid.*, pp. 11, 12.

CHAPTER V

DARBY'S DOCTRINE OF ESCHATOLOGY

EVEN A CASUAL READING of Darby's prophetic interpretations reveals how deeply contemporary dispensationalism is rooted in them. This is not to say that they are identical in all details, or that there has been no further development since Darby's time. But the basic elements, and the hermeneutical pattern, of Darby's eschatology persist unchanged in contemporary dispensationalism.

Darby's writings stand in sharp contrast with traditional views on eschatology. His spirit of independence from the scholarship of the past is best reflected by one of the opening statements in his prophetic writings.

> For my own part, if I were bound to receive all that has been said by the Millenarians, I would reject the whole system: but their views and statements weigh with me not one feather. But this does not hinder me from inquiring by the teaching of the same Spirit . . . what God has with infinite graciousness revealed to me concerning His dealing with the Church.
>
> I confess I think the modern writers on prophecy justly chargeable with following their own thoughts hastily, and far too removed from the control of the Scripture . . . . They take some text or prophecy as a starting point, pursue these suggestions of their minds in connection with their general views previously adopted, but leave the results almost entirely untried by the direct testimony of the Word, affording us theories . . . diverging into the absurdities. . . . *There is not a single writer whose writings I have seen (unless it be the author of one short inquiry) who is not chargeable with this fault.*[1]

Immediately after the context of the statement above, he writes, "I shall take notice . . . of some things which seem to me to be illustrative of the ungrounded, unscriptural statements

---

1. J. N. Darby, *Reflections Upon the Prophetic Inquiry, and the Views Advanced in It*, Col. Writ., Pro. Vol. I, pp. 6. 7. Italics added.

many of which, I think have dishonoured Scripture, and been spoken ignorantly. . . ."[2] The points he mentions are: the spiritual interpretation of the heavenly Jerusalem; the ignorance of the true nature of the Gentile and Jewish dispensations; the role of the Gentiles in the millennium; the distinction between God's kingdom and Christ's earthly reign upon the throne of David; and the restoration of Paradise during the millenium. Throughout his other prophetic writings, often repeated, are references to other traditional views which reflect a basic disagreement with his own dispensational Israel-oriented literal eschatology.

Darby's eschatology grows out of two basic principles: his doctrine of the church, which is itself rooted in his dispensational dichotomy between Israel and the church; and a hermeneutical application of rigid literalism, particularly to prophetic Scripture.

He refers to the "hinge upon which the subject and the understanding of Scripture turns" as the distinction between "Jewish and Gentile dispensations."[3] In applying his literal interpretation he states,

> There are two or three principles which I would lay down. . . . First, in prophecy, when the Jewish church or nation (exclusive of the Gentile parenthesis[4] in their history) is concerned, i.e., when the address is directed to the Jews, there we may look for a plain and direct testimony, because earthly things were the Jews' proper portion. And, on the contrary, where the address is to the Gentiles . . . there we may look for symbol, because earthly things were not their portion, and the system of revelation to them must be symbolical. When therefore the facts are addressed to the Jewish church as a subsisting body . . . *I look for a plain, common sense, literal statement as to a people with whom God had direct dealing upon earth, and to whom He meant His purposes concerning them to be known.* . . . Secondly, intimately connected with this . . . is another principle, viz., that wherever history affords

2. *Loc. cit.*
3. *Ibid.,* p. 27.
4. This statement written in 1830 is, to the author's knowledge, the first time this phrase had been applied to the church. In referring to the church, Darby writes, "this present time is called . . . a parenthesis . . . sixty-nine of Daniel's weeks are run out, and then there is an interval of ages, and the last week begins again." J. N. Darby, *The Dispensation of the Fulness of Times,* Col. Writ., Cri. Vol. I, p. 236.

the history of a fact, there we may expect it to be distinctly and literally declared as predicted in prophecy.[5]

Though it is doubtful whether Darby followed the principle of symbolizing references to the "Gentile," i.e., the church (since he often literalized references to it), there is no doubt whatsoever that he applied it unvaryingly to Israel. Every reference, every promise, every prediction was given rigidly literal interpretation. Literal interpretation became synonymous with valid interpretation. Naturally this affected his general eschatological outlook, since symbolism is an inherent part of prophecy. Applying rigid literalism to virtually every reference to Israel necessarily brought his thought into conflict with contemporary eschatological interpretation, as we may infer from his repeated references to "answers to" and "opposition to" his view.

That the dichotomy between Israel and the church was paramount in Darby's eschatological thought is reflected in his statement that:

> . . . the great object of prophecy . . . is, the combat which takes place between the Second Adam and Satan. It is from this center of truth that all light which is found in Scripture radiates. This great combat may take place either for the earthly things . . . and then it is in the Jews; or for the Church . . . and then it is in the heavenly places. *It is on this account that the subject of prophecy divides itself* into two parts: the hope of the Church, and those of the Jews. . . .[6]

A summary of the chronology of his eschatology reveals the extent to which his thought developed. Beginning with the basic premises of the covenantal obligations of God, he views the nation of Israel as temporarily set aside because of its rejection of its Messiah, His kingdom being postponed, and the church now becoming "something altogether apart — a kind of heavenly people. . . ."[7] The rights of the Messiah, however, have not been set aside. Even though His kingdom has been postponed, even though He now has a heavenly people (the church, in contrast to His earthly people, Israel),

5. J. N. Darby, *On "Days" Signifying "Years" in Prophetic Language*, Col. Writ., Pro. Vol. I, pp. 53, 54.

6. J. N. Darby, *The Hope of the Church of God in Connection With the Destiny of the Jews and Nations, As Revealed in Prophecy*, Col. Writ., Pro. I, p. 567.

7. *Ibid.*, p. 572.

and, even though He will glorify His Church, He will do so without "abandoning any of His rights upon the earth."

Israel had been the called of God, and was promised a government upon the earth. Israel's failures caused it to be incapable of manifesting the principles of the government of God, hence the government was transferred to the church, which exercises it by calling out some from the nations to be a heavenly people. Nevertheless, Israel continues to be the called people, "for the gifts and calling of God are without repentance."

When the church is raptured out of the earth to its heavenly existence, Israel and the nations of the world will be left. The nations will be under the influence of the antichrist, and Israel will join him in an alliance. Tribulation comes from the great wrath of Satan, who is released upon the earth, but a remnant of Israel will await the coming of the King. Then Christ will return with His church after the tribulation to establish His terrestrial kingdom and claim the rights given to Him through the covenants as the seed of David.

Here the literalism of Darby is displayed. Christ will purify the "land" — from the Nile to the Euphrates — of all wicked people so that Israel may possess her "promised land." Then Jesus will reveal Himself to the Jews: "not as the Christ from heaven, but as the Messiah of the Jews." Israel will accept Him as the Messiah, the Kingdom will be established, the wicked one will be cut off, and the Jews will be at peace in their land.

> Those who have seen the glory manifested in Jerusalem will go and announce its arrival to the other nations. These will submit themselves to Christ; they will confess the Jews to be the people blessed of their Anointed, will bring the rest of them back into their land, and will themselves become the theatre of glory, which, with Jerusalem as its center, will extend itself in blessing wherever there is man to enjoy its effect. The witness of the glory being spread everywhere, the hearts of men, full of goodwill, submit themselves to the counsel and glory of God in response to this testimony. All the promises of God being accomplished, and the throne of God being established at Jerusalem, this throne will become to the whole earth the source of happiness.[8]

8. Darby, *The Hope of the Church*, pp. 579-580. This summary of Darby's eschatology is taken from a lengthy article consisting of eight lectures on eschatology.

This summary reflects again the dichotomy of the system — that there is a different *hope* for the church and for Israel. The hope for the church is that it will share in Christ's glory, both earthly and heavenly. The hope for Israel is the kingdom on earth with Christ seated on the throne of David. Each must be considered now in detail.

The Earthly Glory of the Church

Promise of this earthly glory is abundant in Scripture. Colossians 3:4 pledges, "When Christ, who is our life, shall appear, then shall ye also appear with him in glory." John 14:3 promises, "I will come again and receive you unto myself, that where I am there ye may be also," and I Corinthians 15:51 asserts, "We shall not all sleep, but shall all be changed." This is the entrance of the church into its glory as taught by I Thessalonians 4:16, 17, "The Lord himself shall descend from heaven with a shout, with the voice of an archangel, and with the trump of God; and the dead in Christ shall rise first: then we which are alive and remain shall be caught up together with them in the clouds, to meet the Lord in the air; and so shall we ever be with the Lord."

There is, moreover, a special resurrection of the Church.[9] The believing saints will be resurrected before the unbelieving dead, for, as a part of Christ's body they occupy a special place in God's plan, and are destined to share Christ's glory with Him. "In the passages concerning the resurrection, not one speaks of a simultaneous rising of the just and unjust; and those which refer to the resurrection of the just speak of it as a thing distinct."[10] There will be a resurrection of both the just and unjust, but they will not take place at the same time, as is attested in I Corinthians 15:51, 52, where it distinctly states that only the "incorruptible" shall be raised; I Thessalonians 4:16, where the dead "in Christ" shall rise; Luke 14:14, which refers to the "resurrection of the just"; and Revelation 20:6, where there is a reference to participating in the "first resurrection."

The Holy Spirit is the distinctive element in this resurrection, for the just (the church) are resurrected to share Christ's

9. J. N. Darby, *The Two Resurrections*, Col. Writ., Doc. Vol. III, p. 559.

10. Darby, *The Hope of the Church*, p. 463.

glory, while the unjust, who remain in the unresurrected state, await judgment. The resurrection of the church is a unique aspect of God's plan, for, having been buried with Him by faith in baptism and regeneration, the church has already been resurrected, in God's mind, with Christ, and now awaits the time when it shall be resurrected *in fact*, to be with Him. When He returns to receive His inheritance over the earth, the church, because it is one with Him, will be raised to receive His inheritance. The unjust have no part in this resurrection for they will be raised, not for glory, but for judgment.

> At the coming of Christ, these [the church] will rise as regards their bodies, by His Spirit that dwells in them Rom. viii:11. This is that resurrection — not of judgment, but of life (John v. 29) — which belongs to the church by virtue of her union with Christ by the Holy Ghost. It cannot therefore concern the wicked; although they also must be raised up in their own time by the word of Christ, but to be judged. Those who belong to Christ will be raised at His coming; as for the rest of the dead, their resurrection will take place when Christ, after having delivered up the kingdom will be seated, as Son of man, on the great white throne, to judge the dead. . . .11

The interval between the two resurrections cannot be dogmatically determined. The period is mentioned only in Revelation 20:5 as a "thousand years." The uncertainty concerning the lapse of time, however, is altogether independent of the principle involved: the resurrection of the just, the church, occurs at the coming of Christ when the church will be raptured to reign with Him in glory, while the unjust await judgment at the end of the church's reign of earthly glory.

This resurrection introduces the church to a new relation to Christ. Prior to the rapture the church has only a theoretical relation of being risen with Him; it has been in the process of being gathered. At this resurrection, however, it will be bodily and literally ushered into the immediate presence of Christ — into a new relation of glory, with Christ literally as its head. It will be united to Christ in the "marriage of the Bride to the Lamb."12

It is this distinctive fact that constitutes the hope of the church — the final union of the church to Christ to share with

11. J. N. Darby *The Purpose of God,* Col. Writ., Pro. Vol. I, p. 417.
12. J. N. Darby, *Notes on the Revelation,* Col. Writ., Pro. Vol. II, p. 379.

Him all praise and tribute of His glory.[13]　The church will become a partaker of His nature (II Peter 1:4) ; will receive with Him the homage of all creation; will judge fallen angels and the apostate world; and will be the "servants and instruments who will dispense the light and blessings of His kingdom over an earth delivered of all its sorrows, and where Satan is no longer."[14]

This new relation of glory will be established when Christ returns for His church.　The dead in Christ and the living saints will be caught up in secrecy "to ever be with the Lord" (I Thess. 4:17).　"The church goes to join the Lord in the heavenly places . . . [where] salvation will be consummated in the seat of glory itself, from whence she will return with the Lord in glory and power."[15]　This does not constitute a return to the earth by Christ, but merely an "appearing" for His church, that, having received its inheritance of glory through its heirship as the body of Christ, it may return with Him when He comes to the earth to appear visibly and personally before all men.

When the church is translated into the "heavenly places" to receive its inheritance through Christ, "there will follow the battle in heaven . . . that the seat of government may be purged. . . ." Satan will be dispossessed and cast down to the earth "having great wrath because he knoweth he hath but a short time."　Power will be established in heaven according to the purpose of God, but evil will grow rampant upon the earth under the antichrist, who, inspired by Satan, will enter into a civil-ecclesiastical government with the Jews, and a time of great tribulation will follow.　Christ, returning with His glorified church, will put down the antichrist; Satan will be bound; and a remnant of Israel will be established again under the unconditional promise of the covenant with Abraham.　Christ will establish His perfect reign over the earth, taking over the government established by the antichrist.　At the end of a "thousand years" Satan will be loosed for "a little season," and, deceiving the nations, will cause them to rebel against the rule of Christ.　He will be cast into the lake of

13. J. N. Darby, *The Church, What Is Her Power, Hope, Present Position and Occupation?* Col. Writ., Evan. Vol. I, p. 570.

14. Darby, *The Purpose of God*, pp. 416-17.

15. Darby, *Notes on the Revelation*, p. 379.

fire; the unjust will be resurrected for judgment; after which the advent of the new heaven and new earth will begin.[16]

When Christ returns to the earth with His church, His object of judgment will be the rejection of His love by men and the renewal of the covenant with Israel.

> Once the gospel has run its course, Christ will demand righteous judgment against the world. It is no longer Christ, at the right hand of the Father, sending down the Holy Ghost to gather together His co-heirs; but Christ calling for righteousness and asking it . . . against proud and violent men.[17]

In the midst of this devastating judgment, however, the church is securely united to Christ in His glory. Its place is to be with Christ, to enjoy the intimacy of His love and care, and to be protected from all danger by His presence. No harm will affect it, for it is wedded to Christ as His Bride, and will receive the deference and respect of the world which is due its position.

> "The Lord my God shall come, and all the saints with thee . . ." [Zechariah 14:5b]; when He shall have presented His spouse to Himself, a glorious church, "without spot or wrinkle or any such thing," in her own beauty and glory that is proper to herself, seeing in her the beauty and glory of the Father, and with Him in His own glory, and in the power of the love in which He has loved her, and given Himself for her, that she might be perfectly purified and glorious with Him where He is; and then brought forth in glory with honors such as His, the participator in all His glory, the glory given Him of the Father . . . to judge angels and the world; companions in all His glory, and the ministers and instruments of the light and blessings of His reign over a refreshed and solaced earth. . . .[18]

The consequence of this return will be the acknowledgment of "every tongue" and "every knee" that He is the Lord supreme. Evil will cease, peace and true liberty will reign without interference, all God's promises will be fulfilled, His right-

16. J. N. Darby, *Thoughts on the Revelation*, Col. Writ., Exp. Vol. II, pp. 474-612; *Lecture on the Second Coming of Christ*, Col. Writ., Pro. Vol. IV, pp. 384, 466-512; *The Hope of the Church*, pp. 574-80; *Notes on Revelation*, pp. 375-84; *Synopsis of the Bible*, Vol. V (Revelation); *Notes on the Apocalypse*, Col. Writ., Pro. Vol. II, pp. 1-165.

17. Darby, *The Hope of the Church*, p. 511.

18. J. N. Darby, *Divine Mercy in the Church*, Col. Writ., Pro. Vol. IV, p. 196.

eous demands satisfied, and Christ glorified. It will be a reign of glory — and the church is to share it with Christ![19]

The scope of this glory is limited only by the glory of Christ — a limit beyond human comprehension, for Christ shall receive *all* glory. The church will inherit the glory due to Christ as creator and as risen Lord. When He executes judgment over the iniquitous earth, the church will be His chief instrument of justice (Revelation 19)[20]; when He reigns over the earth made righteous by His holiness, the church will share that holiness (Jude); when He receives the praise and tribute of "every knee" and "every tongue," the church as His Bride will share His supremacy (Zechariah 14); when He executes judgment upon the unjust at the last resurrection, the church will share the vindication of His death; and when He returns to the Father, having established the new heaven and new earth, He will usher the church into a new and everlasting glory — to share His heavenly glory.[21]

The Heavenly Glory of the Church

The glory which the church will share with Christ on the earth is purely transitory; its ultimate hope of glory is with Christ in heaven. Gaining this glory will be but the realization of its true character and destiny, which is to be united with Christ in heaven.[22]

It is true that its present character is earthly, as the witness of Christ on earth, but this is as to fact, not title. The church is in a transitory state, being gathered as the body of Christ, built up as the habitation, but when it is complete it will join Christ in heaven, clothed with the same glory as its Head. As the earthly form of the body of Christ it is earthly in nature, but its true character is heavenly, and its ultimate destiny will be to realize, in fact, its heavenly character.

The hope of the church is identified with, and founded on, the relationship in which it is placed as united to the Lord Jesus Christ in heaven, for He is the center of her existence. It is not merely the hope of the individual, but of Christ's

19. J. N. Darby, *General Remarks on the Prophetic Word*, Col. Writ., Exp. Vol. II, p. 248.
20. Darby, *Lectures on the Second Coming*, p. 377.
21. Darby, *Divine Mercy in the Church*, pp. 194-96.
22. J. N. Darby, *Churches and the Church*, Col. Writ., Eccl. Vol. IV, p. 482.

body — a corporate hope. Even while on earth as a pilgrim, it is the Bride of Christ, theoretically seated with Him in heaven and waiting to be with Him actually in heaven. It will remain on the earth, with an earthly character, until all things are set right in His kingdom, but this is not its hope, for "her hope, as her actual association, is with the Lord Jesus Christ in heaven, where she knows Him."[23]

Her assurance of a heavenly glory lies in her heavenly character. Established on earth as a "heavenly economy" to assure the continuance of Christ's ministry, it has the "spirit of promise, which is the earnest of its inheritance, until the redemption of its purchased possession," and has the assurance that, when conformed to the image of Christ in heaven, it will receive its heavenly privileges.[24]

Initiation of its heavenly glory will begin at the "marriage of the Lamb," when it is caught up to be with Him. Salvation, which has been theoretically perfected in Christ, will be consummated by the union of Christ to His Bride — the body being made complete, and the habitation finally erected. At that moment the church will enter its glory, its true character will be manifested, and its theoretical position made factual.

> The spiritual blessings in heavenly places which we enjoy even now in hope, and hindered in many ways, will be for us, in that day, things natural, our physical and normal state, so to speak.[25]

> We shall be there with the Lord, ever with Him: no interruption, no decay of joy, but rather even increasing delight. . . . We are with Him in that place, with Himself, and with Him in the joy, infinite joy, which He has in the Father's love, a love resting on Him as Son, but in His excellency as such, loved before the world was, and now the accomplished of redemption.[26]

Two aspects of this heavenly glory are clearly discerned: as it relates to the kingdom on earth, and to the powers of heaven.

When Christ returns to the earth after the "marriage" union

23. J. N. Darby, *The Church, What Is It?*, Col. Writ., Eccl. Vol. III pp. 560-71.

24. J. N. Darby, *Christ's Coming, Faith's Crowning*, Col. Writ., Exp. Vol. VII, p. 124.

25. Darby, *The Hope of the Church*, pp. 436.

26. J. N. Darby, *The Hope of the Christian*, Col. Writ., Prac. Vol. I, p. 343.

with the church to vindicate His holiness over the earth, the church will return with Him in the joy of its heavenly glory.[27]

> . . . the earth will not fail to feel the effect of it. "Wicked spirits in heavenly places," (see margin Eph. vi. 12) whose place will be then filled by Christ and His church, will cease to be the continual and prolific causes of the misery of a world subjected to their power by sin. The Church, on the contrary, with Christ, reflecting the glory in which she participates, and enjoying the presence of Him who is at once to her its source and fulness, will beam upon the earth in blessing; and the nations of those who are saved will walk in her light. "Help meet for Him" in His glory, full of thoughts of her beloved, and enjoying His love, she will be the worthy and happy instrument of His blessings, whilst, in her condition, she will be the living demonstration of their success.[28]

When Christ returns to heaven in great glory and power, after His personal reign of righteousness over the earth, the church will return with Him in its heavenly glory to take its place at His side forever, and to share with Him the praise of the heavenly hosts. Two aspects of this heavenly glory are prominent: the church will *share* glory given to Christ; and it will *contribute* to His glory. Angels, principalities, and powers will be subjected to Him, and the church will share fully with Christ in the receipt of their praise.[29] It will contribute to the glory of Christ through its own praise to Him as its Head, through its love, obedience, and fellowship with Him as the eternal object of His grace. It will "fill the heavenly places with its own joy. . . ."[30] The height of this joy will be the consummation of the church's love to Christ in a complete and continuing worship of Him for His sacrifice,[31] when, with all hindrance removed, the Bride offers herself completely to the Bridegroom.

No one will deny that Darby's description of the glory which the church will share with Christ is an inspiring hope. The soul rejoices in anticipation of such glory. There are, how-

---

27. J. N. Darby, *Brief Remarks on the Work of the Rev. David Brown, D.D., Entitled, "Christ's Second Coming, Is It Pre-Millennial?"* Col. Writ., Pro. Vol. IV, p. 566.

28. Darby, *The Hope of the Church,* p. 437.

29. Darby, *Divine Mercy in the Church,* pp. 186-87.

30. Darby, *The Hope of the Church,* p. 580.

31. J. N. Darby, *On Worship,* Col. Writ., Doc. Vol. II, p. 181.

ever, some aspects of his eschatological chronolgy which bear evaluation, particularly the events connected with the coming of the Lord. It is difficult from our perspective of having heard this chronology so many times to grasp the significance of it in the theology of Darby. When he enunciated the concept of a special resurrection of the church, a rapture at the appearing and a later return *with* the Lord, and a Jewish millennium as a literal fulfillment of the promises to Abraham, he was introducing a new concept into the thought of the church. Apart from his contemporaries and a tentative suggestion of it in others, the church had not known such doctrine. We must remember that these doctrines arose out of the dichotomy of the church—Israel relation, and the principle of literal interpretation, neither of which was a part of the historic faith of the church.

The Hope of Israel

While much of the hope of Israel has already been contrasted with that of the church, a summary of Darby's concepts about Israel is in order.

God's plan from the beginning of the covenant has been to establish the kingdom. The unconditionalness of the promise obligates God to do so — in fact, He will do so to vindicate Himself before the world. All of His actions with Israel have been pointed toward the kingdom. Merely because Israel rejected the kingdom does not alter God's plan.

The return of Christ to the earth to establish the kingdom, therefore, is the hope of Israel. The kingdom will be literal; the nation will occupy the land, the temple will be rebuilt, the sacrifices reinstituted, Christ will sit upon the throne of David, and Israel will be acknowledged by the nations of the world to be the favored people of God. A millennium of national sublimity will be established!

This will grow out of the remnant who will come out of the tribulation, who will acknowledge Jesus as the Jewish Messiah. The gospel of the kingdom will be preached, and Israel as a nation will accept Jesus as the rightful heir to the throne of David. Once accepted, Jesus will establish the mediatorial kingdom, from which the glory of Israel will radiate.

Darby emphatically declares about this mediatorial kingdom that it will be the literal fulfillment of the covenantal obligations; that it is distinct from the church or the Kingdom of God; that it is the same kingdom which Jesus offered to Israel during his earthly ministry; that it will establish Israel in prominence over all other nations, and that it has always been in the mind of God.[32]

32. The eschatology of contemporary dispensationalism reflects its affinities to Darby's thought. The scope of Darby's prophetic contributions to it may be seen in the titles of some of his writings: *The Dispensation of the Kingdom of Heaven; The Personal Reign of Christ on Earth During the Millennium; The Passing Away of the Present Dispensation; Divine Mercy on the Church and Toward Israel; The Hope of the Church, in Connection with the Destiny of the Jews and the Nations; The First Resurrection; Judgement of the Nations; Israel's First Entry Into the Land Was the Result of the Promise; Israel's Failure and Dispersion; Promises of Restoration; Inquiry as to the Antichrist of Prophecy; Signs of Antichrist: Elements of Prophecy In Connection with the Church, the Jews and the Gentiles; What Saints Will be in the Tribulation; The Rapture of the Saints and the Character of the Jewish Remnant; Are There Two Half-Weeks in the Apocalypse: The Coming of the Lord and the Translation of the Saints,* and many studies on Daniel and Revelation.

CHAPTER VI

EVALUATION AND IMPLICATIONS FOR CONTEMPORARY CHURCH LIFE

NO EVALUATION of these backgrounds to dispensationalism can be adequate unless it touches upon three basic ideas: Darby's personal contribution to its genesis; its conception of the heavenly church; and the adequacy of its hermeneutical principles. While an evaluation of these ideas is important, their implications for contemporary church life are even more important.

Darby's Personal Contribution

Part of Darby's contribution to dispensationalism is that he created an atmosphere out of which the system grew. This study has already demonstrated that both his theology and this atmosphere were a departure from the traditional concepts of the church. Dispensationalism grew out of the Brethren movement, or Darbyism, as it is sometimes called, and much of its character and spirit has developed as the direct result of the personal magnetism of the man. His impact on the movement, for good or bad, is universally admitted: no man contributed more to it than he did.

Whatever may be said about Darby's spirit in later life, one inevitable fact towers above all others: at the beginning he was the personification of the saintly life. When he left the Established Church he did so in a spirit of true humility, genuinely longing for a more spiritual fellowship. During the early days at Plymouth his spirit of unselfishness was an example of holy, loving fellowship in unity, contributing to the general atmosphere of a pure community in Christ. His personal magnetism, intellectual acumen, marked spiritual maturity, as well as his position as one of the leading organizers, made him prominent in Brethren circles. A transformation of character and purposes seems gradually to have taken place,

141

so that his loving unselfish nature changed to one of personal ambition, leaving him with a dual personality in which he retained some of his early simplicity of soul but to which an antagonistic and ambitious spirit had been added.

The influence of Darby's personality can be traced through the subsequent history of Brethrenism, which began as an effort to secure a spiritual fellowship where all men might gather under the theme "The Blood of the Lamb and the Union of the Saints." Ignoring doctrinal differences and ecclesiastical views, tolerant of all differences of opinion, united on the principle of open ministry and the privilege of all saints to break bread, Brethrenism soon changed to the point of claiming for itself the *exclusive* title of the church of God on earth, arrogating to itself the right to treat all Christians outside its narrow fellowship as "outside the church of God on earth because outside of that which represents it."[1] Its fellowship was shattered by strife and controversy, its unity was broken by theological disputes, and its Table was denied to many merely on the ground of their friendships and associations. Responsibility for this melancholy spectacle lies almost wholly with Darby.[2]

His dominating spirit, most vividly demonstrated in his controversy with B. W. Newton, molded the character of Brethrenism and changed the principles upon which it was founded. His word became the law of discipline, withering out spiritual affections, fostering enmity and pride, changing allegiances, and introducing a spirit of party strife. His demands for strict adherence in doctrine and practice reduced the liberty of free and independent evaluation on the part of most of his followers, who often either feared or refused to use their power of discernment and blindly followed his lead. His unrelenting pursuit of his object caused bitterness among friends, disrupted close associations, and, in general, broke the pure ground of fellowship upon which the Brethren had met, making the atmosphere of controversy almost inseparable from the movement.

1. As attributed to Mr. Goodall in the Walworth-Sheffield discipline. Quoted from a letter by Darby to a Mr. Spurr, as quoted by W. Blair Neatby, *A History of the Plymouth Brethren*, p. 225.

2. The doctrine, spirit, and practices of the Brethren of Darby's era should not be automatically attributed to the Brethren of today, for many modifying tendencies have tended to expunge some of his extreme views.

The extent to which this party spirit disrupted the purity of its fellowship is illustrated by W. H. Cole, who, after commenting on the loving fellowship which existed at the beginning, refers to the effect of the controversy.

> This devastating work began soon after Mr. J. N. Darby's return from the continent in 1845. I was told that, when he left Plymouth for his mission there, he commended Mr. B. W. N. to the assembly as one qualified to lead on the saints in truth . . . and to watch over, and guide them in all spiritual matters. But when he returned he found him in a position of great influence, attracting to his teaching believers from various parts of England, many of whom took up their residence in Plymouth, to benefit by his teaching and that of others. What were the feelings this popularity stirred? It would not perhaps be difficult to suppose, but a personal attack was soon made, and the disastrous strife of the two great teachers, who then became rivals, broke up the peace of the assembly and almost stopped the progress of the work . . . . no account, gathered merely from pamphlets, could describe the distress of mind, the poignant sorrow and heart grief produced by Mr. D. as he ruthlessly pursued his course against his former friend. . . . I deeply regret to have to record that strifes, jealousies, wraths, factions, parties, works of the flesh, took the place in great measure of the fruit of the Spirit, and loving fellowship of the saints.[3]

Darby was also undoubtedly the maker of Brethrenism as a theological system, and he gave it the impetus it needed for expansion. He systematized its doctrinal position, and through his own dynamic personality, intellectual capabilities, and social position, popularized the movement. His fearlessly crusading spirit, as well as his logical insight into spiritual matters, presaged and caused its rapid expansion, until in the space of but a few years its testimony was internationally felt.

His theology was the root out of which dispensationalism grew. He developed the basic doctrinal pattern and hermeneutical principles which have been carried through to contemporary dispensationalism. What modifications that have been made since his day have been in detail only — the principles remain unchanged. Others have amplified his views, but no dispensationalists have ever repudiated their basis in his thought.

One can only imagine what the total impact of Brethrenism

3. W. H. Cole, as quoted by G. H. Lang, *The Local Assembly*, pp. 75-76.

would have been had this man retained the spirit of humble service to the body of Christ which he exhibited in the mountains of Wicklow County and had not introduced his theological extremes, nor exerted his personal despotism, but with equal zeal had given to the world the fellowship and spiritual truth which was known at Dublin in the early days.

Has not the history of dispensationalism demonstrated, however, that the spirit of Darby has characterized its development? Certainly the personal recriminations of Darby's bitter and caustic attacks on those who disagree is not a feature of the movement today. Is there still not, however, a subjective feeling that all who do not accept the dispensational truth, particularly the pre-tribulation rapture, do not really believe in the blessed hope? Have not entire denominations become divided over this very issue, with dispensationalists pressing the issue of "modernism" against those who reject their doctrine? Has not history demonstrated that dispensationalism is a divisive element in the Christian church?

There are dispensationalists, of course, who maintain fellowship with the brethren who disagree with them, and do so in a loving spirit. Anyone, however, who is aware of the circumstances through which this movement has developed — from its inception in the Brethren controversies, through the struggle for prominence in the prophetic conference movement, and in its fight for survival today, will have to admit that it has had a disruptive influence upon the church. This spirit of divisiveness must be attributed largely to the influence of Darby — not only in the example of his personal vindictiveness, but in his insistence that any theology disagreeing with his own was unbiblical. Paradoxically, his own system was itself a departure from historic premillennialism.

The Heavenly Church

The "heavenly church" idea in dispensationalism comes from several sources. These include an exegesis of passages concerning the church, particular the Ephesian references, which contrast the church with the earthly Israel; Darby's church-in-ruins concept, which led him to teach that Christendom is apostate; and a strong emphasis on the doctrine that the church is in the world, but not of the world.

Darby's own practice suggests, however, that ecclesiastical

expediency contributed significantly to his formulation of this doctrine. By maintaining staunchly that the existing church organizations were forsaken by God in favor of "heavenly assemblies," which in turn included only those who receive the truth as he conceived it, Darby put himself in a position to advance his own program.

Contemporary dispensationalism does not hold the "assembly truth" of Plymouth Brethrenism, of course. Is not the attitude of a "pure" church in the midst of an apostate Christendom still an integral part of the dispensational view, however? Does not this concept tend to make dispensationalists withdraw from fellowship with members of the larger Body of Christ, particularly if the latter do not hold dispensational truth? Has not this concept of inclusive purity narrowed the field of fellowship in the church?

One may further question whether Darby's teaching that the church must separate itself from evil was not inspired by his wish to gain personal authority. He gained this authority by simply declaring that deviations from his leadership were evil. He failed to realize, however, that unity is not necessarily uniformity. Because he identified the two, he failed to realize that the spiritual unity of the body can co-exist with differences of doctrine and practice.

Contemporary dispensationalists do not officially take Darby's extreme view as their own. Nevertheless, in practice they suggest that strict doctrinal conformity is a prerequisite of Christian fellowship. While it would be grossly oversimple to state that dispensationalists are wholly responsible for evangelical separatism today, their presupposition that Christendom is apostate does encourage this tendency. Certainly the problem is complicated by the fact that many churches have abandoned *cardinal* doctrines of the Christian faith; nevertheless, dispensationalists usually insist upon *far more* than these cardinal doctrines as criteria of the true church.

The reader will, of course, have to interpret from his own experience whether this is a true analysis of the spirit of dispensationalism. Happily, there are many dispensationalists who do not reflect this spirit. Unhappily, many others do. From his own experience and study the author most reluctantly concludes that the divisive spirit is an inherent part of the system, to the detriment of the total Body of Christ.

The dispensationalist emphasis on the Jewish millennium, particularly with its teaching of the pre-tribulation rapture in order that the remnant of Israel may be gathered, all but replaced belief in historic premillennialism during the first part of this century.[4] Whether Darby actually originated the idea of the secret rapture is certainly open to question. Thomas Croskery[5] suggests that it was derived from the thought of Pierre Lambert, a Jesuit priest. LeRoy Froom[6] suggests that it came from Franciso Ribera, another priest. More probably, however, its origin can be traced through the Irvingite movement. Darby and Irving both attended the Powerscourt conference,[7] over which Darby exercised leadership. Irving may have come to the view first, although Daniel Fuller suggests that

> it would have been possible for both Darby and Irving to come to these views independently of one another, and since it will be demonstrated that the pre-tribulation rapture must be granted if the concept of the two people of God be accepted, it is concluded that the safest course to take is that Darby originated the idea from his own hermeneutical premises.[8]

Fuller's inference here is that Darby's general hermeneutical and prophetic patterns were well established by the time of the Powerscourt conferences, and since the two are so closely related, he must have held them prior to this. He adds,

4. C. Norman Kraus, *Dispensationalism in America*. Richmond: John Knox Press, 1958, p. 104. After tracing the conflict in the prophetic conferences of the late nineteenth century between the dispensational views and the historic pre-millennial view, Kraus concludes, "[By] 1901 . . . the dispensationalists had won the day so completely that for the next fifty years friend and foe alike largely identified dispensationalism with premillennialism."

5. Thomas Croskery: *Plymouth-Brethrenism*: *A Refutation of its Principles and Doctrines*. London and Belfast: William Muller and Sons, 1879, p. viii.

6. Froom, *The Prophetic Faith of Our Fathers*, III, 655ff.

7. Sponsored by Lady Powerscourt, a prominent member of the Plymouth Brethren. There is a reference in her *Letters and Papers of the Late Theodosia A. Viscountess Powerscourt*, ed. Robert Daly (London, A. S. Rouse, 1895), to a romantic relation with Darby, which he probably abandoned because of his work. This probably accounts for his prominence at the prophetic conferences held at her castle, although his spirit of dominance would certainly be a factor.

8. Daniel P. Fuller, *The Hermeneutics of Dispensationalism* (unpublished doctoral dissertation at Northern Baptist Seminary, Chicago, Illinois, 1957), p. 54.

The propriety of such a course is further borne out by the fact that Darby claimed that this doctrine came to him from a new insight into the Scriptures: "It is this passage [II Thess. 2:1, 2] which twenty years ago [i.e., from 1850 when he wrote] made me understand the *Rapture* of the saints *before* — perhaps a considerable time before — the Day of the Lord [that is, before the judgment of the living]."[9]

Whether the view originated with Darby is really not important, however. What is important is that he integrated it into a basic pattern of interpretation, and systematized it into a prophetic doctrine which he promulgated. He may not have originated it, but he certainly introduced it into the main current of prophetic interpretation.

Now bear in mind that the "Brethren" . . . were beginning to form into an assembly in 1829 — just seven years after Irving came to London, and that about 1833 this doctrine of the rapture before the tribulation began to be put forth in Lady Powerscourt's meetings, where all these hungry souls, seeking for primitive simplicity and power, congregated, and that after a time Mr. Darby became the herald of the new view. . . .[10]

The fact that it was distinctive of Darby's doctrine is further substantiated, as Alexander Reese[11] points out, by the resistance offered to it by some of the other early Brethren leaders: Tregelles, Newton, Muller, and others. It is significant that though ". . . Darby made the study of prophecy the pivot of his work; and his delineations of millennial glory dazzled the minds of his hearers,"[12] Tregelles, one of the great textual scholars of the nineteenth century, never accepted the pretribulation rapture idea, while remaining in Brethrenism.

As has been demonstrated previously, this view introduced

9. *Ibid.*, p. 54. Darby's statement comes from William Kelly's *The Rapture of the Saints: Who started it, or rather on what Scripture?* The very title suggests the innovation of a new concept in the theology of the church.

10. Robert Cameron, "A Letter to Friends of Prophetic Truth," *Watchword and Truth*, XXIV, August, 1902, p. 238, and quoted by Fuller, *op. cit.*, p. 53. Kraus, *op. cit.*, p, 46, quotes Cameron as referring to this as introducing "a theory without a single advocate in all the history of the Church, from Polycarp down" (Cameron, "Prophetic Teacher," *Watchword and Truth*, XVIII, October, 1896, p. 258).

11. Alexander Reese, *The Approaching Advent, An Examination of the Teaching of J. N. Darby and His Followers*. London: Marshall, Morgan & Scott, Ltd., n.d., p. xi.

12. Neatby, *op. cit.*, p. 81.

a new concept into prophetic interpretation. Representative scholars such as Nathaniel West[13] and Charles Maitland,[14] two of the nineteenth century's most reliable analysts of prophetic trends, trace a premillennarian view from the earliest times of the primitive church, with various interpretations of the first resurrection of the saints before the millennium, but neither of them, as completely and thoroughly as they have traced its history, find any belief in a secret pre-tribulation rapture. Both of them show that premillennial scholars in general have interpreted the first resurrection to be concurrent with the personal return of the Lord to the earth.

The implications go deeper than this, however. Belief in a pre-tribulation rapture tends to alter one's concept of the *purpose* of the church in the world. Dispensationalists, who insist that the purpose of the church is to call out the "heavenly body" from the world, and that this body will be ultimately raptured *away from* tribulation, have forgotten that the church was placed *in* the world so that through it Christ's message might come *to* the world.

The church does have a responsibility to the culture in which it finds itself. This responsibility involves communicating the teachings of Jesus so that they will have an impact upon the moral and social problems of society. The church is in the world for more than merely calling out a heavenly body: it has a mission *to the world* itself.

The mission of the church to the world is to reflect the ethics and ideals of Jesus, through personal salvation, into the culture of society so that that culture may be changed. The principles of the Sermon on the Mount must be translated by the church into practical principles of Christian living. This is not to suggest that the church will ever ameliorate the sinful world to the extent that it becomes a perfect society, but it is to emphasize that the church cannot escape its mission by repeating that it is "not of the world and not for the world." Dispensationalism would withdraw the church from its impact upon the world, contending, as does the Scofield Bible, that

13. Nathaniel West, "History of the Pre-Millennial Doctrine," *Premillennial Essays of the Prophetic Conference*. Chicago: F. H. Revell, 1879, pp. 332ff.

14. Charles Maitland, *The Apostles' School of Prophetic Interpretation, With Its History Down to the Present Times*. London: Longman, Brown, Green & Longman, 1849.

". . . the Sermon on the Mount in its primary application gives neither the privilege nor the duty of the Church,"[15] because it is a part of the gospel of the kingdom.

Has not the evangelical church all too long defaulted the proclamation of the gospel to the "world"? Does not God yearn for His church, which has the true gospel, to carry the message of this gospel to the problems of the culture in which it lives? Has not dispensationalism contributed largely to this default of the church's mission, and made of it a detached, withdrawn, inclusively introverted group, waiting to be raptured away from this evil world?

Is it too much to ask the evangelical church of today to stand in its world and let Christ minister through it to the world? The church needs to throw off the mantle of "in but not of" detachment and apply itself vigorously to the spiritual and social problems of its world.

The Hermeneutical Principle of Literalness

The basic implications of dispensationalism arise, not out of its chronology of eschatological events, but out of its principle of literal interpretation.

It takes a courageous (or foolish) evangelical commentator to question the principle of literal interpretation today, particularly since for most of evangelicalism "literal" has become synonymous with "valid." In questioning dispensationalist hermeneutics, I should like it understood in the most emphatic terms that I accept the principle of verbal inspiration of Scripture. I stand squarely in the center of the Reformation theology on the veracity of Scripture as contained in the canon of the Bible.

I cannot resist questioning, however, whether all prophetic Scriptures should be interpreted literally. Dispensationalism stresses technical definitions of terms as the basis of its hermeneutics. We must not forget, however, that there is more to interpretation than discovering the meaning of words. Prophetic interpretation must proceed in the light of context, the mood of the author, the conditions to which he is writing, and the over-all pattern of the Scriptures. Not all prophetic Scripture can be interpreted literally.

15. *Scofield Reference Bible,* p. 999, f.n. 2.

Dispensationalism, however, insists that *all* prophetic Scripture must be taken literally. C. I. Scofield, whose synthesis of Darby's principles forms the core of contemporary dispensational hermeneutics, contrasts the difference between historical and prophetic Scripture as follows: historical Scriptures are literally true, but may have an *allegorical* or *spiritual* significance; prophetic Scriptures are always literal and may *never* be interpreted otherwise.

> . . . they [historical Scriptures] have [perhaps more often than we suspect] an *allegorical* or spiritual significance. Example, the history of Isaac and Ishmael. Gal. iv. 23-31 . . . It is then permitted — while holding firmly the historical verity — reverently to *spiritualize* the historical Scriptures. [In prophetic Scriptures] . . . we reach the ground of *absolute literalness*. Figures are often found in the prophecies, but the figure invariably has a literal fulfillment. Not one instance exists of a "spiritual" or figurative fulfillment of prophecy . . . Jerusalem is always Jerusalem, Israel is always Israel, Zion is always Zion. . . . Prophecies may never be spiritualized, but are always literal.[16]

This is an important declaration of interpretative principle. Scofield is no extremist, out in the periphery of dispensationalism. His interpretation of Darby's principle forms the guide line for dispensational hermeneutics. *Not one representative dispensationalist has ever, to this author's knowledge, repudiated the principles he enunciates above;* to do so would be to repudiate the very foundation on which dispensationalism is built.

This principle, when applied consistently, has two implications: it involves the dispensationalist in some extreme interpretation, and it separates him from the historic premillennial faith.

Logically carried out, this principle involves the dispensationalist in these extremes: all Israel (presumably every Israelite) will be saved; the boundaries of the land given in the promise to Abraham will literally be restored during the millennium; Christ will return to a literal, theocratic, political kingdom on earth with a government patterned after existing national governments, with David as his regent: Christ will sit on a physical throne in the city of Jerusalem, in the state of

16. C. I. Scofield, *Scofield Bible Correspondence Course,* Chicago: Moody Bible Institute, pp. 45-46.

Israel; the beast, Antichrist, and other persons mentioned in Revelation will literally appear; a city will actually descend from heaven,[17] in which God will have an eternal throne, and from which will flow the river of life — all of which are inherent in the system of contemporary dispensationalism.

It is true, of course, that literal interpretation of obviously literal prophecy is to be preferred. But a system of hermeneutics which requires *all* prophecy to be interpreted with absolute literalism is committed to forced exegesis.

If, however, we reject absolute literalism as the universal rule of interpretation of all prophecies, how are we to know how to interpret *any* prophecy? Floyd Hamilton appears to be correct when he says that one should follow the literal rule unless (a) the passages contain obviously figurative language, or (b) unless the New Testament gives authority for interpreting them in other than a literal sense, or (c) unless a literal interpretation would produce a contradiction with truths, principles, or factual statements contained in non-symbolic books of the New Testament, and (d) to allow the clearest New Testament passages in non-symbolic books to be the norm for the interpretation, rather than obscure or partial revelation contained in the Old Testament.[18]

In the light of this principle, it is legitimate to ask whether dispensationalism is not oriented more from the Abrahamic Covenant than from the Cross. Is not its focus centered more on the Jewish kingdom than on the Body of Christ? Does it not interpret the New Testament in the light of Old Testament prophecies, instead of interpreting these prophecies in the light of the more complete revelation of the New Testament?

Does dispensationalism not become involved in forced exegesis when, for example, it attempts to evade the New Testament's equation of the church with the seed of Abraham? What literal interpretation can it give to these clearly enunciated passages from the New Testament: "They are not all Israel, that are of Israel: neither, because they are Abraham's seed, are they all children: but, in Isaac shall thy seed be called. That is, it is not the children of the flesh that are children

17. Notice Walvoord's description of its literal dimensions on page 46.
18. Floyd Hamilton, *The Basis of the Millennial Faith*. Grand Rapids, Wm. B. Eerdmans Publ. Co., 1955, p. 53,

of God; but the children of the promise are reckoned for a seed" (Rom. 9:6-8) ; "Now to Abraham and his seed were the promises made. He saith not, And to seeds, as of many; but as of one, And to thy seed, which is Christ. . . . For ye are all the children of God by faith in Christ Jesus . . . There is neither Jew nor Greek . . . for ye are all one in Christ Jesus. *And if ye be Christ's, then are ye Abraham's seed, and heirs according to the promise*" (Gal. 3:16, 26, 28, 29) ; "They that are of faith, the same are the sons of Abraham" (Gal. 3:7) . How can these passages be interpreted consistently, and literally, if one does not conclude that there is a closer unity between the church and Israel than the dispensational dichotomy between the two allows?

May not the answer be found in the fact that the church is indeed the spiritual Israel; that the covenantal relations of God to Israel have indeed passed over to the church; that the promises to Abraham may be fulfilled in some measure in the church; that the kingdom offered by Christ was a spiritual kingdom which was instituted in the hearts of those who believe; that the church is neither a parenthesis nor an intercalation, but the cumulative display of God's total redemptive plan; that the millennium is to be a personal reign of Christ over a spiritually oriented kingdom rather than a theocratic, Jewish oriented one; that the blessed hope is the return of Christ, rather than the rapture of the church, and that the grace of God is indeed the principle by which *all* men of *all* periods are brought to God.

John P. Milton summarizes a way out of the dispensational dichotomy:

> In the light of the New Testament the exaggerated emphasis on land and nation instead of on the promise of blessing seems like a religious anachronism. To substitute the millennium for the gospel as the interpretative key to Scripture will save no one, nor will it solve anything. The love of Christ might find a way; a political claim to Palestine based on a faulty Scriptural exegesis never will. . . .
>
> Israel was not called to be an end in itself, but a means to an end; to be a servant of God through whom we have received the Sacred Scriptures as the Word of God, and Jesus Christ according to the flesh as the Saviour of the world. Jesus Christ and the Church which is His body is the fulfillment: not an accidental afterthought, but the intended goal from the beginning; the fulfillment of the

vocation of Abraham to be a blessing and of Israel to be a kingdom of priests, and a holy nation (Exodus 19:6). Significantly, the very words of the latter passage (Exodus 19:5-6) are applied to the Church in I Peter 2:9-10: "But you are a chosen race, a royal priesthood, a holy nation, God's own people (or, a people for his possession), that you may declare the wonderful deeds of him who called you out of darkness into his marvelous light. Once you were no people but now you are God's people; once you had not received mercy but now you have received mercy" (see also vs. 4-5). And the words of Paul in Ephesians 1 concerning "every spiritual blessing in the heavenly places" in Christ, in whom we are "destined and appointed to live for the praise of his glory," with the Holy Spirit as "the guarantee of our inheritance in hope until we acquire possession of it," is more than a superficial reflection of the similar language in the Old Testament: it is the fulfillment of it. . . . The New Testament is constantly drawing out the deep spiritual implications of that which was said and done, of history and of prophecy, in the Old Testament.[19]

The most profound implication of dispensationalism, however, goes even beyond its hermeneutics or chronology. The sum total of all its doctrines tends to make it a separatist, withdrawn, inclusive theology. The idea that "all down the ages, the true children of God have been forced, either by the claims of conscience or by the teaching of Scripture (as they see it), into positions of isolation from the mass of their fellow-believers,"[20] may be true if this isolation is from the open evil of ungodliness, but it is tragically wrong if it separates the Body of Christ.

Is not the true church wider in scope than the separatist movements of twentieth-century evangelicalism have been willing to admit? Is not the *unity* of the larger fellowship in Christ more inclusive than the restricted corners of isolationism into which some segments of evangelicalism have withdrawn themselves? Is not the fellowship which can be shared in a mutual understanding about the nature and redemptive mission of Christ more important than a restrictive fellowship that centers in a narrowly defined eschatological doctrine?

The world awaits Christ's community, the church. It awaits

19. John P. Milton, *Prophecy Interpreted*. Minneapolis: Augusburg Publ. House, 1960, pp. 59, 58.
20. Harold St. John, *The Church*, (J. B. Watson, ed.), London: Pickering & Inglis, Ltd., 1949, p. 197.

with its frustrations, fears, complexities, and doubts. The church exists to stand in prophetic judgment against the injustice, disharmony, arrogance, greed, pride, unbrotherliness, and sin of the world. Any theological system which causes a part of the church to withdraw from the larger fellowship in Christ and, by isolationism and separatism, to default its role, is wrong.

EPILOGUE

The theses of this book are: dispensationalism is not a part of the historic faith of the church; it is not the only premillennial view, since there was a historic premillennial interpretation for eighteen centuries before dispensationalism was formulated; and, it is based on a faulty hermeneutical basis of interpretation. I will have to leave to the judgment of the reader whether I have proved my points.

There is another point which needs to be made, however. In spite of some extremities in this system, it does emphatically enunciate the truth that Jesus is to return to earth personally, literally, and actually in the Second Advent. So does historic premillennialism. So also does amillennialism. These may differ as to the chronology of the events surrounding this blessed hope of the church, but all three views share in the one essential emphasis which the writers of the New Testament also share — that Christ will return!

Having this central truth in common, adherents to all these three views should be able to have fellowship in love and tolerance. Eschatological interpretations may differ, and should be debated sharply to find the truly biblical principle, but should not be made a test of fellowship.

I strongly differ with my dispensational brethren in their interpretation, but would defend their right to adhere to their view. I believe it to be a faulty one, but will not separate from fellowship with any who disagree with me. I ask only that the same tolerance be afforded to those who disagree with them.

While maintaining fellowship in love, I most strongly believe dispensationalism to be a departure from the historic faith and to be based on a faulty system of interpretation. I am bold enough, therefore, to believe that if I have demonstrated my theses, many dispensationalists will think through to a new evaluation of their eschatological system of thought, as I have had to do.

PREFACE TO BIBLIOGRAPHY

The accompanying list of books represents a selected bibliography of Darby's writings on the church, and of books, pamphlets, articles, and tracts on the history of Brethrenism. The bibliography is divided into four sections: the writings of Darby on the church (which are, in turn, divided into Historical, Ecclesiological, and Eschatological) ; the history of Brethrenism; contemporary dispensationalism; and contemporary non-dispensationalism.

The paucity of primary materials concerning Brethrenism, added to the fact that there is no known collection of these materials, makes research on the history of the movement difficult. In order that the effort which the author has expended in locating the materials contained in this study may not be lost, he has elected to include in this bibliography the sources from which they may be obtained, and these are indicated by the use of a symbol following each book. Where possible, the pressmark for library copies is included. Since Brethrenism originated in Britain there is no known American collection of works pertaining to its early days. The Emmaus Bible Institute of Oak Park, Illinois, has a scanty collection of the early tracts.

Key to the sources are indicated as:
    NCL — New College, Edinburgh
    ULE — University Library, Edinburgh
    NLS — National Library of Scotland, Edinburgh
    EPL — Edinburgh Public Library, Edinburgh
    BML — British Museum Library, London
    ELL — The Evangelical Library, London
    MPL — Middlesborough Public Library, Middlesborough
    BLO — Bodleian Library, Oxford
    MFL — Manchester Free Library, Manchester

In addition to the books listed here, the reader will find much material for doctrinal study on Brethrenism in the library of the late William Kelly, which is now housed in the Middlesborough Public Library, though it contains little concerning the historical aspect of the movement. Its 15,000 volumes contain a rich treasury for theological studies.

The author has not presumed upon the generosity of those private collectors who have so graciously allowed him access to their libraries, by publicly listing such information in this bibliography, inasmuch as he has not obtained their permission to do so.

BIBLIOGRAPHY

I. THE WRITINGS OF J. N. DARBY ON THE CHURCH

Darby, John Nelson, *The Collected Writings of J. N. Darby*, edited by William Kelly. London: G. Morrish, 1867-83, 32 Vols.

These *Collected Writings* are divided into eight categories, which with their symbols are indicated below as: Eccl. — Ecclesiastical; Doc. — Doctrinal; Exp. — Expository; Pro. — Prophetic; Prac. — Practical; Cri. — Critical; Evan. — Evangelistic; and Apol. — Apologetic.

For purposes of this study, there follows a selected bibliography of J. N. Darby's writings on the church. It is divided into Historical, Ecclesiological, and Eschatological.

HISTORICAL

Account of Proceedings at Rawstrone Street, in November and December, 1846, with an Answer to the "Reasons" Circulated in Justification of the Refusal of Mr. Newton to Meet the Brethren. Eccl. VI, 122.

The Bethesda Circular. Doc. IV, 233.

Indifference to Christ: or Bethesdaism, Extracted from a Private Letter. Eccl. IV, 311.

Letter to the Saints Meeting in the Ebrington Street on the Circumstances which Have Recently Occurred There. Eccl. IV, 100.

Letter on the Confession of Error by Some. Eccl. IV, 301.

Letter of Acknowledgement as to Plymouth. Eccl. IV, 308.

Letter to the Rev. Mr. Guers on the Subject of His Notes on the Errors of Mr. B. W. Newton. Doc. IV, 265.

Narrative of the Facts, Connected with the Separation of the Writer from the Congregation Meeting in Ebrington Street. Eccl. IV, 1.

Summary of the Meetings in London. February, 1847, Eccl. IV, 270.

Two Letters as to Plymouth. Eccl. IV, 287.

To the Brethren at Rawstrone Street. Eccl. IV, 290.

What Investigation Has There Been at Plymouth. Eccl. IV, 254.

ECCLESIOLOGICAL

An Appeal to the Conscience of Those Who Take the Title of "Elders of the Evangelical Church at Geneva," and a Reply to One of Them. Eccl. II, 471.

A Few Remarks Connected With the Presence and Operation of the Spirit of God in the Body, the Church. Doc. I, 491.

A Glance at Various Ecclesiastical Principles and Examination of the Foundations on which Institutions of the Church on Earth are Sought to be Based — in Reply to Various Writings. Eccl. II, 1.

A Letter to the Saints in London As to the Presence of the Holy Ghost in the Church. Doc. I, 525.

A Letter to Count du Gasparin in Answer to a Question Which He puts to Me in the "Archives du Christianisme." Eccl. II, 521.

A Letter on Separation. Eccl. I, 534.

A Short Answer to the Last Article by Count du Gasparin, Published in the "Archives du Christianisme." Eccl. II, 574.

A Short Reply to "Landmarks," No. 6 of the S.P.C.K. Doc. IX, 462.

Are You Praising With Christ? Prac. I, 390.

Brethren and Their Reviewers. Doc. III, 67.

Brief Notice of the "Record's" Comment on "J.N.D.'s" Letter. Doc. IX, 144.

Brief Remarks on the Spirit and the Assembly. Eccl. IV, 545.

Christ's Association of Himself With His People on Earth. Exp. II, 89.

Christ in Heaven and the Holy Spirit Sent Down. Doc. IX, 371.

Christ on High and the Holy Ghost Here Below. Evàn. II, 227.

"Christ Loved the Church." Exp. VI, 239.

Christianity Not Christendom. Doc. V, 379.

Christian Liberty of Preaching and Teaching the Lord Jesus Christ. Eccl. I, 103.

Churches and the Church. Eccl. IV, 479.

Church and Privileges. Doc. IX, 426.

Considerations Addressed to the Archbishop of Dublin and the Clergy Who Signed the Petition to the House of Commons for Protection. Eccl. I, 1.

Considerations of the Nature and Unity of the Church of Christ. Eccl. I, p. 30.

Considerations on the Character of the Religious Movement of the Day and on the Truths by which the Holy Ghost Acts for the Good of the Church. Eccl. II, 123.

Correspondence on Recent Matters. Doc. IX, 559.

Discipline and Unity of the Assembly. Eccl. IV, 381.

Disendowment-Disestablishment: a Word to the Protestants of Ireland, in a Letter to the Venerable Archdeacon Stopford. Eccl. IV, 436.

The Doctrine of the Church of England at the Time of the Reformation Itself, of Scripture, and of the Church of Rome, Briefly Compared with the Remarks of the Regius Professor of Divinity. Doc. I, 1.

Ephesians. Eccl. IV, 490.

Extract from a Letter, in Reply to some Questions on the Lord's Supper. Eccl. IV, 427.

Episcopacy: What Ground Is there in Scriptrue or History for Accounting It an Institution of God? Eccl. IV, 463.

Examination of a Few Passages of Scripture, the Force of which has been Questioned in the Discussion on the New Churches; with Remarks on Certain Principles Alleged in Support of Their Establishment. Eccl. II, 349.

Familiar Conversations on Romanism: The Word of God and the Church. Doc. VI, 1.

Fellowship and the Right State For It. Doc. IX, 554.

Grace and Government. Exp. VI, 210.

Grace, the Power of Unity and of Gathering. Eccl. I, 558.

God's House and Way. Evan. II, 66.

God, Not the Church, the Teacher by His Word: being a Letter on Dr. Manning's Sermon. By a Stranger Passing through Hereford. Eccl. IV, 338.

Letter to a Christian Friend, in Reply to a Presbyterian Minister, on the Subject of the Law, The Sabbath, Ministry and the Sacraments. Eccl. III, 531.

Matthew XVI. Eccl. III, 153.

Notice of the Statement and Acknowledgement of Error Circulated by Mr. Newton. Doc. IV, 181.

On the Apostacy. What is Succession a Succession of? Eccl. I, 170.

On Discipline. Eccl. I, 517.

On Ecclesiastical Independency. Eccl. III, 57.

On the Formation of Churches. Eccl. I, 211.

On Gifts and Offices in the Church. Eccl. III, 1.

On Lay Preaching. Eccl. I, 200.

On Ministry: Its Nature, Source, Power, and Responsibility. Eccl. I, 315.

On the Presence and Action of the Holy Ghost in the Church: In Answer to the work of Mr. P. Wolff, entitled, "Ministry as Opposed to Hierarchism and Chiefly to Religious Radicalism." Doc. I, 316.

On Worship. Doc. II, 133.

Observations on a Tract, entitled "Plymouthism in View of the Word of God." Eccl. II, 415.

Observations on "A Statement from Christians in Ebrington Street." Doc. IV, 196.

Operations of the Spirit of God. Doc. I, 11.

Parochial Arrangement Destructive of Order in the Church. Eccl. I, 122.

Principles of Gathering. Doc. IX, 576.

Power in the Church: or, Not Imitation, But Obedience in the Sense of Present Ruin. Doc. IX, 450.

Presbyterianism: a Reply to "The Church and the Pulpit." Eccl. III, 483.

Remarks on the Pamphlet of Mr. F. Olivier, entitled, "An Essay of the Kingdom of God, followed by a Rapid Examination of the Views of Mr. John Darby." Eccl. I, 426.

Remarks on the State of the Church in Answer to the Pamphlet of Mr. Rochat, entitled, "A Thread to Help the Simple to Find their Way." Eccl. I, 357.

Remarks upon "The British Churches in Relation to the British People," by E. Miall. Eccl. III, 468.

Remarks on a Book entitled, "Is Modern Christianity a Civilized Heathenism?" Eccl. IV, 442.

Remarks on Second Timothy. Eccl. IV, 550.

Remarks on the Presence of the Holy Ghost in the Christian. Doc. I, 483.

Remarks on "The Church and the World." Doc. IV, 461.

Reply to Judge Marshall's Tract on the Tenets of the Plymouth Brethren (So-Called). Eccl. IV, 409.

Reply to the Defense of the Doctrine of Baptismal Renegeneration by the Bishop of Assory, Leighlin and Ferns. Eccl. IV. 409.

Reply to the Remarks in Two Leading Articles of the Christian Journal, entitled, "Our Separating Brethren." Eccl. III, 176.

Reply to Two Fresh Letters from Count du Gasparin, Published in the "Archives du Christianisme," of December 23, 1854, and February 24, 1855. Eccl. II, 530.

Review of a Sermon, Preached by the Rev. G. M. Innes, in the Quebec Cathedral, on Sunday, April 5, 1868, and published in the "Quebec Mercury," April 9. Eccl. III, 369.

Separation From Evil God's Principle of Unity. Eccl. I, 538.

Scriptural Unity and Union. Doc. VII, 467.

Scriptural Views Upon the Subject of Elders — in Answer to a Tract, entitled, "Are Elders to be Established?" Eccl. II, 280.

Some Further Developments of the Principles set forth in the Pamphlet, entitled, "On the Formation of Churches," and Reply to Some Objections Made to Those Principles. Eccl. I, 238.

The Apostacy of the Successive Dispensations. Eccl. I, 189.

The Character of Office in the Present Dispensation. Eccl. I, 140.

The Christ of God, the True Center of Union. Doc. IV, 259.

The Christian Not of This World. Doc. IX, 335.

The Claims of the Church of England Considered; being the Close of Correspondence Between the Rev. James Kelly, of Stillogan, Ireland, and J. N. Darby. Eccl. III, 267.

The Church — the House and the Body. Eccl. III, 138.

The Church and its Friendly Subdivisions — in Reply to Mr. R. W. Monsell. Eccl. II, 202.

The Church, Which Is His Body: a Letter on A.R.D.'s Few Thoughts as to the Position of the Saints Gathered in the Name of the Lord. Eccl. IV, 317.

The Church — What Is It? Her Power, Hopes, Calling, Present Position, and Occupation. Evan. I, 557.

The Church in the Wilderness in the Vision of God. Evan. I, 528.

The Church an Habitation of God Through the Spirit. Evan. I, 325.

The Church of Christ. Crit. I, 578.

The Gospel and the Church According to Scripture: Being a Review of "Church Doctrine, Bible Truth," by the Rev. M. S. Saddler. Doc. VIII, 491.

The House of God, the Body of Christ; and the Baptism of the Holy Ghost. Eccl. III, 23.

The Notions of a Clergyman Dispensationally the Sin Against the Holy Ghost. Eccl. I, 54.

The Presence of the Holy Ghost on Earth Consequent on Christ's Exaltation to the Right Hand of God. Evan. II, 145.

The Two Ministries. Evan. II, 357.

The Sabbath. Is the Law Dead Or Am I? Doc. III, 424.

The Saints Praise as Taught and Led by Christ. Prac. II, 460.

The Will of God, the Work of Christ, and The Witness of the Holy Ghost. Evan. II, 575.

Thoughts on the Church. Eccl. IV, 511.

What Is the Church? Doc. I, 551.

What Is the Unity of the Church? Eccl. IV, 447.

What the Christian Has Amid the Ruin of the Church; being a Reply to Certain Articles in the "Jamaica Magazine." Eccl. III, 413.

What Has Been Acknowledged? or, the State of the Controversy About Elders; Followed by a Short Answer to an Article of Mons. de Gasparin. Eccl. II, 438.

What is the Church, as it was at the Beginning? and what is its Present State? Eccl. III, 115.

What Is a Sect? Eccl. III, 550.

ESCHATOLOGICAL

A Brief Notice of a Tract, entitled, "Remarks on the Seventh Chapter of Daniel." Pro. III, 577.

A Few Brief Remarks on "A Letter on Revelation XII." Pro. IV, 36.

A Letter Addressed to —, Parsontown, in Reply to a Tract, entitled, "Three Considerations; Proving Unscriptural the Supposition of the Personal Reign of Christ on Earth During the Millennium." Pro. I, 113.

An Examination of the Statements Made in the "Thoughts on the Apocalypse," by B. W. Newton; and an Enquiry into How Far They Accord With Scripture. Pro. III, 1.

Answer to a "Letter to the Brethren and Sisters Who Meet for Communion in Ebrington Street." Pro. III, 491.

Answer to a "Second Letter to the Brethren and Sisters Who Meet for Communion in Ebrington Street." Pro. III, 526.

Are There Two Half Weeks in the Apocalypse? Pro. IV, 256.

"As Is the Heavenly." Prac. I, 516.

Brief Analysis of the Book of Daniel. Pro. IV, 83.

Brief Remarks on the Work of Rev. David Brown, D.D., entitled, "Christ's Second Coming: Is It Pre-Millennial?" Pro. IV, 513.

Brief Thoughts On the Apocalypse. Pro. IV, 293.

Christ's Coming, Faith's Crowning. Exp. VII, 122.

Christ the Hope, and the Holy Ghost, with our Responsibility. Evan. II, 221.

Coming of the Lord. Apol. I, 405.

Divine Mercy in the Church and Towards Israel. Pro. I, 185.

Elements of Prophecy, in Connection With the Church, the Jews, and the Gentiles. Pro. IV, 62.

Enquiry as to the Antichrist of Prophecy. Pro. II, 331.

Evidence From Scripture of the Passing Away of the Present Dispensation. Pro. I, 136.

Examination of the Book, Entitled, "The Restoration of All Things." Doc. IX, 114.

General Remarks on the Prophetic Word. Exp. II, 242.

Grace Rejected, and Heavenly Glory Opened. Prac. I, 419.

"I Will Come Again." Exp. VI, 456.

Is the Coming of Christ For His Saints the Proper Hope of the Church? Doc. III, 404.

Judgement Seat of Christ. Doc. VII, 556.

Lectures on the Second Coming of Christ. Apol. I, 466.

Messianic Prophesies. Apol. I, 466.

Notes on the Apocalypse. Pro. II, 1.

Notes on the Revelation. Pro. I, 250.

On "Days" Signifying "Years" in Prophetic Language. Pro. I, 48.

On the Extended Scope of Prophecy. Pro. I, 65.

On the Apocalypse. Exp. 505.

Outline of the Revelation Pro. II, 358.

Outline of the Revelation. Exp. VII, 541.

Our Joy in Heaven. Prac. I, 415.

Questions of Interest as to Prophecy. Pro. II, 349.

Remarks on a Part of Daniel. Pro. II, 324.

Remarks on the Seven Churches. Pro. II, 387.

Remarks on Three Tracts, entitled, "Signs of the Coming of the Lord: For Whom Are They Given." Pro. IV, 1.

Reflections Upon the Prophetic Inquiry and the Views Advanced In it. Pro. I, 1.

Seven Lectures on the Prophetical Addresses to the Seven Churches. Pro. II, 393.

Short But Serious Examination of the Fundamental Principles Issued by Mr. Gaussen in His Book, entitled, "Daniel the Prophet." Pro. IV, 95.

Studies on the Book of Daniel. Pro. II, 191.

Substance of a Lecture on Prophecy. Pro. II, 166.

The Allusions in "The Last Trump." Cri. I, 564.

The Antichrist, Properly So Called. Cri. I, 560.

The Call of the Bride. Prac. I, 185.

The Coming of the Lord and the Translation of the Church. Pro. IV, 269.

The Coming of the Lord, That Which Characterises the Christian Life. Misc. I, 371.

The Covenants. Doc. I, 68.

The Dispensation of the Kingdom of Heaven Pro. I, 80.

The Force of the "Last Day" in John VI. Cri. I, 563.

The Hope of the Church of God, in Connection with the Destiny of the Jews and the Nations, as Revealed in Prophecy. Eleven Lectures: Pro. I, 420.

    The Church and Its Glory. p. 427.

    The Second Coming of Christ. p. 439.

    The First Resurrection: or, Resurrection of the Just. p. 455.

    Progress of Evil on the Earth. p. 470.

The Two Characters of Evil — Ecclesiastical Apostacy, and Civil Apostacy. p. 487.

Judgement of the Nations, Which Become the Inheritance of Christ and of the Church. p. 506.

Israel's First Entry into the Land Was the Result of Promises. p. 523.

Israel's Failure and Dispersion: Promises of Restoration. p. 536.

Same Subject, and the Manner of Its Accomplishment. p. 551.

Summing up and Conclusion. p. 562.

The Hope of the Christian. Prac. I, 335.

The Marriage Supper of the King's Son. Evan. I. 397.

The Melchisedec Priesthood of Christ. Pro. I, 97.

The Power of Christ in Resurrection and in Glory, or Thoughts on Philippians III and Mark X. Prac. I, 477.

The Principles Displayed in the Ways of God, Compared with His Ultimate Dealings. Pro. II, 587.

The Purpose of God. Pro. I, 401.

The Rapture of the Saints and the Character of the Jewish Remnant. Pro. IV, 179.

The Resurrection. Prac. II, 488.

The Resurrection, the Fundamental Truth of the Gospel. Doc. I, 225.

Thoughts on the Revelation. Exp. II, 474.

The Two Resurrections. Doc. III, 559.

What Do the Scriptures Teach Concerning the Judgment to Come? Doc. III, 581.

"We Have This Treasure." Prac. I, 534.

What Saints Will There Be in the Tribulation. Pro. IV, 166.

What Is the Church. Doc. I, 551.

Letters of J. N. D. London: G. Morrish, n.d., 3 Vols.; London; Stow Hill Bible and Tract Depot, n.d., 3 Vols. NLS 143.d; BML, 20020 ee 53.

Darby, John Nelson. *Synopsis of the Books of the Bible.* London: G. Morrish, n.d., third edition, revised. 5 Vols. EPL., 30139 BS 20: NLS, L 143: BML, 20020 ee 53: BLO, Gh 203.

——. *Spiritual Sons.* Edited by H. A. Hammond. London: James Carter, 1893, Second Edition, Revised. NLS, Bq. 2; BML, 11653.i,11.

——. *Notes and Jottings.* London: Foreign Gospel Tract and Book Depot. n.d. (BML copy destroyed by enemy action.) Not in Col. Writ.

——. *Sermons and Sunday Tracts.* London: G. Morrish, n.d. Not in Col. Writ.

II. THE HISTORY OF BRETHRENISM

A. PRIMARY MATERIALS

Balding, G. *Epitome of the Ramsgate Sorrow. Dates and Facts, With a Few Notes By the Way.* London: G. B. Ferndale RD., Clopham, Surrey, 1882, Second Edition.

Congleton, Lord (J. V. Parnell). *Reasons For Leaving Rawstone Street, London.* Bristol: Wright and Son, 1847.

Congleton, Lord (J. V. Parnell). *The Bath Case: or Who Made the Division at Bath* (publisher not given), 1849.

Dennet, Edward. *Recovered Truths.* London: W. H. Broom, 1866. NLS, L. 55. f.

Dorman, W. H. *High Church Claims of the Exclusive Brethren. A Series of Letters to Mr. J. L. Harris.* London: Morgan and Chase, n.d. BML, 4135 aa 36.

——. *The Close of Twenty-Eight Years of Association with J. N. D.: And Of Fellowship and Ministry Amongst Those Who Adopt His Doctrines Concerning the Sufferings of Christ.* London: Houlston and Wright, 1866.

F. W. H. *The "One Body."* London: James Hawkins, n.d.

——. *What Are the Facts? An Affectionate Appeal to "The Brethren" So Called.* London: James Hawkins, n.d. NCL, A5/b5.

Goodall, — —. *Letters Relating to the Recent Excommunication of Assemblies.* Sheffield: Spurr, 114 West Street, n.d.

Groves, A. G. *Catholic Christianity and Party Communion Delineated.* London: Morgan and Chase, n.d. NCL, A5/b5.

Groves, Mrs. A. N. *Memoirs of A. N. Groves.* London: G. Morrish, n.d.

Groves, Henry. *Darbyism. Its Rise and Development.* London: Houlston and Wright, 1867. BML, 4135 aaa 63.

——. *Memoirs of Lord Congleton.* London: J. F. Shaw, 1884. NLS, 224.f.; BLL; BML, 4956 bb 19.

Hall, P. F. *Discipleship.* London: J. K. Campbell, 1884, BML, 4135 aaa 63.

——. *Grief Upon Grief.* London: J. K. Campbell, n.d.

Herzog, J. J. *Les Frères de Plymouth et John Darby.* Lausanne: Georges Bridel, 1844. BML, 4650 b 13.

Ironside, H. A. *A Historical Sketch of the Brethren Movement.* Grand Rapids: Zondervan Pub. House, 1942.

Kenswick, G. *An Explanation of the Principle and Practices of the Park Street Confederacy.* (Publication date not given.)

Newman, F. W. *Personal Narrative in Letters.* London: Holyoake & Co., 1865.

——. *Phases of Faith.* London: John Chapman, 1850. ULE, Z. 1/10.69; BML, 4907 cc 36.

Newton, B. W. *A Defense in Reply to the Personal Accusations of Mr. Darby.* London: Houlston and Wright, 1845.

——. *A Letter to a Friend Concerning a Tract Recently Published at Cork.* London: Houlston and Stoneman, n.d.

——. *A Statement and Asknowledgement Respecting Certain Doctrinal Errors.* Plymouth: Wright and Son, 1847.

——. *Observations on a Tract.* Plymouth: Wright and Son, n.d.

——. *Prepositions For the Solemn Consideration of Christians.*

——. *Five Letters on Events Predicted in Scripture.* London: Houlston & Sons, 1877.

Oliphant, J. S. *Bethesda Fellowship.* Published privately, 1907.

Philadelphos. *The Basis of Peace, a Supplement to "An Appeal to the Brethren, So-Called," Being Observation on Doctrines Relating to the Person of Christ, on Mr. Darby's View of the Third Class of Suffering of Christ, On the Bethesda Question, Fellowship, etc.* Dublin: Stearn Printing Co., n.d. (Not published, for private circulation only.)

Stoney, J. B. *A Letter to the Brethren in the Lord, Meeting in Queen's Road, Reading.* London: G. Morrish, 1885. BML, 4136 as 18 (7).

Tregelles, S. P. *Five Letters to the Editor of "The Record," On Recent Denials of Our Lord's Vicarious Life.* London: Houlston & Wright, 1864. NCL, A5/b5.

——. *Three Letters to the Author of "A Retrospect of Events that Have Taken Place Amongst the Brethren."* London: Houlston & Sons, 1895, second edition. BML, 4136 aa 41.

Trotter, William. *Bethesda in September, 1857.* London: G. Morrish, 1859. BML, 4139 b 90.

——. *The Whole Case of Plymouth and Bethesda.* London: Gospel Book Depot, n.d. Now published by Stow Hill Bible and Tract Depot, London, under the title, *The Origin of So-Called Open Brethrenism.*

Teritus, (pseud.) *Divers and Strange Doctrines.* Bristol: J. Wright, n.d.

Vigram, George. *A Statement from Christians Associating in the Name of the Lord in Ebrington Street, Plymouth.* London: Houlston & Sons, n.d.

——. *To Those Who Have Read Lord's Congleton's Tract Entitled, Reasons For Leaving Hawstrone Street.* Plymouth: Wright & Sons, 1847.

The authors of the following are *anonymous.*

An Appendix Containing Extracts from Pamphlets and Documents Illustrating the "Retrospect of Events That Have Taken Place Amongst The Brethren." London: B. L. Green, 1849. BML, 4135 e (2).

A Retrospect of Events That Have Taken Place Among the Brethren. London: B. L. Green, 1849. BML, 4135 e (1).

An Admonition to Mr. J. N. Darby on His Charge of "Horrible Doctrine" Against Mr. J. L. Harris, of Plymouth, with a Prefatory Letter to Mr. G. V. Wigram. London: J. Watson, n.d.

Shibboleth, or the New Test of Communion Amongst Certain "Brethren;" A Counter Appeal to the Christians at Bethesda, Bristol, in Answer to G. V. Wigram's Attack on Henry Craik, with Reflections. London: Houlston and Stoneman, n.d.

B. SECONDARY SOURCES

Beattie, David J. *Brethren. The Story of a Great Recovery.* Kilmarnock: John Ritchie, Ltd., 1937. ELL; BML, 2033 g 6.

Broadbent, E. H. *The Pilgrim Church.* London: Pickering and Inglis, 1942, second edition.

Carson, James C. L. *The Heresies of the Plymouth Brethren.* Coleraine: John McCombie, 1862. NCL, A5/b5: BML, 4136 aaa 19.

Croskery, Thomas. *Darbyism; or The Separationist Theory of a Pure Church.* London: James Nisbet Co., n.d.

——. *Plymouth-Brethrenism: A Refutation of Its Principles and Doctrines.* London and Belfast: William Mullan & Son., 1879. NLS, L. 24 e.

Dennet, Edward. *The Plymouth Brethren: Their Rise, Divisions, Practice and Doctrine.* London: Elliot Stock, n.d.

G. *Exclusive Brethrenism. Its Origin and Discipline.* London: Coleridge, 1867. BML, 4135 aaa.

Grant, James. *The Plymouth Brethren. Their History and Heresies.* London: W. H. Guest, 1876, new edition. This volume appeared originally as Vol. II of *Religious Tendencies of the Times,* of the same author and publisher. NCL, A5/b5.

Ironsides, H. A. *A Historical Sketch of the Brethren Movement.* Philadelphia: Lauxriza Bros., 1941.

Lang, G. H. *The Local Assembly. Some Essential Differences Between Open and Exclusive Brethren Considered Scripturally and Historically.* Walsham-le-Willows, Suffolk: the author, 1942, new edition.

Macintosh, Duncan. *The Special Teachings, Ecclesiastical and Doctrinal, of the Exclusive Brethren, or Plymouth Brethren, Compiled From Their Own Writings, With Strictures.* London: Houlston & Sons., 1872, fourth edition. NCL, A5/b5.

Mearns, Peter. *Christian Truth Viewed in Relation to Plymouthism.* Edinburgh: William Oliphant & Co., 1875, second edition. NCL, A5/b5.

Miller, Andrew. *The Brethren, Their Origin, Progress and Testimony.* London: Pickering and Inglis, n.d.

———. *Short Papers on Church History From Apostolic Times to the Twentieth Century.* London: Pickering and Inglis, 1929, Vol. III. NCL, A2/b5.

Neatby, W. Blair. *The History of the Plymouth Brethren.* London: Hodder & Stoughton, 1901. NCL, A5/b5; BML, 4715 df 16.

Noel, Napoleon. *The History of the Brethren.* Denver: W. F. Knapp, 120 W. Maple Ave., 1936. 2 Vols. EPL, /G33247/ BR 5750.

Pickering, Hy, *Chief Men Among the Brethren.* London: Pickering and Inglis, n.d., second edition. NCL, A5/b5.

Reid, William. *Plymouth Brethrenism Unveiled and Refuted.* Edinburgh: William Oliphant & Co., 1880. NCL, A5/b5: EPL, /G2345/ BR 5750.

Rogers, J. G. *Church Systems in the XIX Century.* London: Hodder & Stoughton, 1881, NLS, L. 25f; NCL, C12/a1; BML, 4462 i (1891 edition).

Stokes, G. T. *Plymouth Brethrenism: Its Ecclesiastical and Doctrinal Teachings: With a Sketch of Its History.* London: Hodder and Stoughton, 1874. This book is also published by Seely & Son, London. NCL, A5/b5: BML, 4136 c 3 (22).

Tuelon, J. S. *The History and Teachings of the Plymouth Brethren.* London: Society for Promoting of Christian Knowledge, 1883. NLS, L. 136 b; BWL, 4137 bb 3: NCL, A5/b5.

Turner, *John Nelson Darby: A Biography.* London: C. A. Hammond, 1926. NLS.

Turner, W. G. *John Nelson Darby.* London: C. A. Hammond, 1951, second impression.

Vietch, Thomas Stewart. *The Story of the Brethren Movement.* London: Pickering and Inglis, n.d. ELL; BLO.

Whately, E. J. *Plymouth Brethrenism.* London: Hatchards, 1879. NCL, A5/b5.

C. RELATED SOURCES

Baker, H. P. *Why I Abandoned Exclusivism.* London: Pickering and Inglis, 1930. BML, 03089 e 45.

Cox, John. *An Earnest Expostulation to the Author of High Church Claims of Exclusive Brethrenism.* London: Houlston and Wright, 1869. BML, 4139 aaa 33.

————. *A Refutation of Certain Charges Made by the Brethren.* London: Houlston & Wright, 1867. BML, 4135 aa 26.

————. *Judge Righteous Judgment.* London: Houlston & Wright, 1869. BML, 4139 aaa 36.

————. *"Made Like Unto His Brethren."* Manchester-Square: George Hunt, n.d.

————. *Test Before You Trust, or, The Innovation of the Brethren.* London: Houlston & Wright, n.d.

————. *Test Before You Trust, or, The New Doctrine and the Old Divinity Compared.* London: Nisbet & Co., n.d.

Croskery, Thomas. *Catechism of the Doctrines of the Plymouth Brethren.* London: Nisbet & Co., 1866.

Culverhouse. *Observation on the Discipline Amongst the Brethren.* London: Pewtress & Co., 1860.

D. A. *Darbyism: An Attack Upon J. N. D.* London: Cookhead, Bayswater, 1881.

D. E. *Memorials of the Ministry of G. V. Wigram.* London: W. H. Broom, 1870. 3 Vols. NLS, L. 79 h (Vol. II is second edition).

D. J. *A Brief Notice of a Few of P.F.H., W.H.D., and Mr. Gilpin's Questions and Statement, and J.N.D.'s Explanation.* London: G. Morrish, 1867. BML, 4135 e 8 (4).

Davis, C. J. *Helps for Enquirers.* Edinburgh: Robertson, n.d.

Dyer, A. S. *Sketches of English Nonconformity.* London: J. Masters & Co., 1893. BML, 4109 aa 42.

G. *An Enquiry As to the Scriptural Position of the Plymouth Brethren.* London: G. Morrish: Glasgow: R. L. Allen, 1875. BML, 4135 e 3 (8).

G. A. *An Earnest Appeal in a Letter to the Plymouth Brethren. By a Former Member and Deserter.* London: Houlston & Wright, 1867. BML, 4135 aaa.

Gregory, J. R. *The Gospel of Separation.* London: Charles Kelly, 1894. BML, 4139 a 12 (4).

Guiness, H. Grattan. *A Letter to the Plymouth Brethren on the Recognition Of Pastors.* London: Nisbet & Co., 1851.

Henderson, W. T. *A Simple Reply to "A Second Familiar Conversation About the Plymouth Brethren."* London: Allen & Jones, 1865. BML, 4135 aa.

Houlston, Thomas. *Plymouthism and Revivalism or, the Duty of Contending for the Faith in Opposition to Preaching Errors and Corruption.* Belfast: C. Aitchison, 1874, second edition. NCL, A5/b5.

Howard, J. E. *A Caution Against the Darbyites, With a Word to the Author of Two Recent Pamphlets and the Testimony of Lord Congleton.* London: G. T. Stevenson, 1866. NCL, A5/b5.

Hunter, David. *Plymouthists and Their Principles.* Belfast: Bible Colportage Society of Ireland, 1870. NCL, A5/b5.

Ireland, H. *The Principles and Practices of the "Brethren."* Edinburgh: Andrew Elliot, n.d. third thousand. NCL, A5/b5.

Lang, G. H. *Anthony Groves Norris.* London: Thynne & Co. Ltd., 1939. BML, 20029 bb 43.

Latimer, W. T. *Lectures on the Doctrines of the Plymouth Brethren.* Belfast: James Cleeland, 1890. BML, 4139 bbb 23 (2).

M. C. *Plymouth Brethrenism Tested by the Word of God.* London: Eliot Stock, 1881. BML, 4372 df 12 (11).

Miller, A. *Plymouthism and the Modern Churches.* Toronto: William Briggs, 1900. BML, 4182 df 5.

Murdock, Alexander. *Life Among the Close Brethren.* London: Hodder & Stroughton, 1890. BML, 4136 aa 33.

R. T. *"J. N. D.," A Sketch of Some of His Recent Doctrines, a New Testament Emendation.* London: Allen, n.d.

Rees, A. A. *A Friendly Letter to the Christians Called Brethren.* London: Passamore and Alabaster, n.d.

———. *A Second Friendly Letter to the Christians Called Brethren.* London: Passamore and Alabaster, n.d.

Roborough (pseud.). *"Everyday Saints," Sketches from the Life of Some of My Friends Among the "Open Brethren."* London: Arthur Stockwell, 1919. BML, 4135 de 3.

Simons, John. *A Letter to a Highly Respected Friend on the Subject of Certain Errors of the Antionomian Kind Which Have Lately Sprung Up in the West of England, and Are Now Making An Alarming Progress Throughout the Kingdom.* London: Hatchard, 1818. ULE, Yd. 5.

Snow, Thomas. *A Reply to a Letter Written by the Reverend John Simons, Purporting to be on the Subject of Certain Errors of the Antinomian Kind Which Have Lately Sprung Up in the West of of England.* London: J. Moyes, 1818. ULE, Yd. 5.

Stables, G. *Answer to a Sermon on Plymouth Brethrenism.* London: James E. Hawkins, 1883. BML, 4372 df 17 (6).

Trench, F. F. *Extreme Views on Religions Doctrines. Their Possible Cause, Probable Consequences and Best Corrections.* London: Nisbet & Co., n.d.

Watson, J. B., editor. *The Church: A Symposium.* London: Pickering & Inglis, 1949.

The authors of the following are *anonymous*:

A By Stander, *Observation Upon a Letter by the Rev. John Simons, Addressed to a Highly Respected Friend Upon Certain Errors of an Antinomian Kind Which Have Lately Sprung Up in the West of England.* London: T. Hamilton, 1818.

A Brief Enquiry Into the Church Position of the Exclusive Section of the Plymouth Brethren. London: Houlston and Wright, 1875. BML, 4139 b.1 (23).

A Few Faithful Remarks on a Tract Entitled, "A Familiar Conversation with a Plymouth Brethren." London: Houlston and Co. 1865. BML, 4135 aa.

An Address to the Plymouth Brethren. London: Hardwick & Co., 1862. BML, 4139 cc.

An Elder. *Prevalent Errors: a Reply to a Lecture by Mr. G. J. Davis Regarding the Opinions of the Party Known as "Brethren."* Aberdeen: A & R Milne, 1871.

Addresses to the Christians Commonly Called Plymouth Brethren, on Liberty of Ministry and Gift. Norwick: Allen & Brown, 1847. BML, 4135 a.

Darbyism and Its New Bible: Taken From an Article Communicated to the "Sword and Trowel." London: W. Mackintosh, 1874. NCL A5/b5: BML 4136 aa: NLS, 1874 33 (9).

Errors of the Darby and Plymouth Sect. London: James Nisbet & Co. 1862 (appeared in "The Record" of August 11, 20, 27, September 3, 10, 19, 22, 1862). NCL, A5/b5; BWL, 4135 aa.

'Exclusivism Unveiled.' A Handbook of Sixteen Questions of the Tenets Particular to Darbyism. London: W. Macintosh, 1872, seventh edition. NLS, 1872 6 (19); NCL, A5/b5; BML, 1892 (6***).

The Fallacies of the Plymouthist and Darbyite Aspersion of the Church of England Analyzed and Answered. London: "Record Office," 1863. BML, 4139 bb.

The New Opinions of the Brethren. London. B. L. Green & Co., 1849.

The Novel Doctrines as Recently Taught in "The Bible Treasury." London: Hatchard, 1857. BML, 3185 a 40.

The Recent Doctrine of the Five. Mr. Darby's New Bible and Its Announcement by One Who Writes on Behalf of Many. London: W. Macintosh, 1868. NCL, A5/b5; BML, 4135 aaa.

D. PERIODICAL ARTICLES

Croskery, Thomas, "John Nelson Darby," *The Catholic Presbyterian Magazine,* (London: Nisbet & Co., edited by W. G. Blackie) 7:440-45. NCL, 38, 7.

Stokes, G. T. "John Nelson Darby," *Contemporary Review* (London: Isbister & Co.), 48:537. EPL, 13116: NLS, p. 1.

——. "J. N. Darby," *Litell's Living Age,* (Boston: Little and Gray), 167:345. EPL, 22408.

——. "Plymouth Brethrenism," *British Quarterly Review* (London: Hodder & Stoughton), 58:378. EPL, AP 5, B86; NLS, U398.

——. "Plymouth Brethrenism," *Congregational Magazine* (London: Jackson Walford), 25:698. NLS, X120 (or) U385.

——. "Plymouth Brethrenism in 1839." *Eclectic Review* (London: Ward & Co.) 69:571; 71:65. EPL, 21989; NLS, P36.

——. "Plymouth Brethrenism and the Christian Ministry," *London Quarterly Review* (London: Elliot Stock) 31:312.

——. "Plymouth Brethrenism and Lay Preaching in Ireland," *London Quarterly,* 27:1. NLS, X96.

——. "Plymouth Brethren and Their Erroneous Doctrines," *Christian Observer* (London: Hatchard & Co.) 62:433. NLS, Vts. 132.

Assorted Articles, *The Bible Treasury: A Monthly Review of Prophetic and Practical Subjects* (London: G. Morrish, Edited by William Kelly) 1856-1906. NLS, X116; BML, PP178f.

Assorted Articles, *The Present Testimony, and Original Witness Revived* (London: W. H. Broom, Edited by George Wigram) 1849-1867; 1867-1873. NLS, X148 (1853, 58, 62, 64 missing); BML, PP 464 b.

E. ENCYCLOPEDIA ARTICLES

Burton, "Plymouth Brethren," *The Catholic Encyclopedia,* XII, 172-73.

Blunt, J. H. "Plymouth Brethren," *Dictionary of Sects, Heresies, and Schools of Thought,* 433.

McCullough, John. "Brethren (Plymouth)," *Encyclopedia of Religion and Ethics,* II, 843-48.

Whitefield, E. E. "Plymouth Brethren," *A Religious Encyclopedia or Dictionary of Biblical, Historical, Doctrinal and Practical Theology,* edited by Philip Schaff, III, 1856-59.

Whitefield, E. E. "Plymouth Brethren," *The New Schaff-Herzog Encyclopedia of Religious Knowledge,* IX, 94.

The authors of the following are *anonymous*:

"J. N. Darby," *Dictionary of National Biography,* 126.

"Plymouth Brethren," *Encyclopedia Britannica,* XVIII, 93.

"Plymouth Brethren," *Chambers Encyclopedia,* X, 808.

III. CONTEMPORARY DISPENSATIONALISM

A. BOOKS

Beckwith, George. *God's Prophetic Plan Through the Ages.* Grand Rapids: Zondervan Publishing House, 1942.

Blackstone, W. E. (W.E.B.) *Jesus is Coming.* New York: Fleming H. Revell Co., 1898.

Brown, Charles E. *The Reign of Christ.* Anderson, Ind.: Gospel Trumpet, Co., 1950.

Chafer, Lewis Sperry. *Systematic Theology.* 8 vols.; Dallas: Dallas Seminary Press, 1948.

———. *The Kingdom in History and Prophecy.* Findlay, Ohio: Dunham Publishing Co., 1943.

———. *Grace.* Chicago: Moody Press, 1945.

———. *Major Bible Themes.* Chicago: Moody Press, 1944.

Feinberg, C. L. *Premillennialism or Amillennialism.* Wheaton, Ill.: Van Kampen Press, 1954.

———. *Israel in the Spotlight.* Wheaton, Ill.: Scripture Press, 1956.

Gaebelein, Arno G. *The Gospel of Matthew.* 2 vols. in 1; New York: Our Hope Press (Van Kampen Press, distributors).

———. *Hath God Cast Away His People?* New York: Gospel Publishing House, 1905.

———. *The Revelation.* New York: Our Hope Press, n.d.

———. *Daniel.* Grand Rapids: Kregel Publication, 1955.

———. *Half a Century.* New York: Our Hope Press, 1930.

Girdlestone, R. B. *The Grammar of Prophecy.* Grand Rapids: Kregel Publications, 1955 (reprint from earlier editions).

Ironside, H. A. *The Lamp of Prophecy.* Grand Rapids: Zondervan Publishing House, 1940.

———. *Notes on Matthew.* New York: Loizeaux Bros., 1948.

Larkin, Clarence. *Dispensational Truth.* Philadelphia: (Published by the author).

McClain, Alva J. *The Greatness of the Kingdom*. Grand Rapids: Zondervan Publishing House, 1955.

Newell, William R. *The Book of Revelation*. Chicago: Grace Publications, 1941.

Pache, René. *The Return of Jesus Christ*. Chicago: Moody Press, 1955.

Pentecost, Dwight. *Things to Come*. Findlay, Ohio: Dunham Publ. Co., 1958.

Riley, W. B. *The Evolution of the Kingdom*. New York: Charles C. Cook, 1913.

Ryrie, Charles. *The Basis of the Pre-Millennial Faith*. New York: Loizeaux Bros., 1953.

Scofield, C. I. *Rightly Dividing the Word of Truth*. Philadelphia: Philadelphia School of the Bible, 1928. (A reprint of the author's original, after an unauthorized and revised edition had been printed by others in 1921.)

———. *Scofield Bible Correspondence Course*. Chicago: Moody Bible Institute, 1907, renewed 1934.

———. *Scofield Reference Bible*. New York: Oxford Press (American Branch), 1909, 1927.

Silvers, J. F. *The Lord's Return: Seen in History and in Scripture as Premillennial and Imminent*. New York: Fleming H. Revell, 1944.

Stanton, Gerald. *Kept For the Hour*. Grand Rapids: Zondervan Publishing House, 1956.

Trotter, W. (and T. Smith), *Eight Lectures on Prophecy*. London: Pickering and Inglis, n.d.

———. *Plain Papers on Prophetic and Other Subjects*. New York: Loizeaux Bros., n.d.

Van Ryan, August. *The Kingdom of God and of Heaven*. New York: Loizeaux Bros., 1946.

Walvoord, John F. *The Return of the Lord*. Findlay, Ohio: Dunham Pub. Co., 1955.

———. *The Rapture Question*. Findlay, Ohio: Dunham Publ. Co., 1957.

Wood, Leon J. *Is the Rapture Question Next?* Grand Rapids: Zondervan Pub. House, 1956.

B. PERIODICALS

Cameron, Robert, "A Letter to Friends of Prophetic Truth," *Watchword and Truth*, xxiv, August 1902.

———. "Prophetic Teachers," *Watchford and Truth*, xviii, October 1896.

Chafer, Lewis S. Dispensationalism," *Bibliotheca Sacra*, Vol. 93, 1936.

Ehlert, Arnold D., "A Bibliography of Dispensationalism," *Bibliotheca Sacra*, Vol. 102, 1945.

Mason, Clarence E., "A Review of 'Dispensationalism' by John Wick Bowman," *Bibliotheca Sacra*, Vol. 114, 1957.

Walvoord, John F. "Israel's Restoration," *Bibliotheca Sacra*, Vol. 103, 1946.

———. "The Abrahamic Covenant and Pre-Millennialism," *Bibliotheca Sacra*, Vol. 108, 1951.

———. "The Doctrine of the Millennium," *Bibliotheca Sacra*, Vol. 115, 1958.

174 *Bibliography*

C. UNPUBLISHED DISSERTATIONS

Cawood, John W. "A Definitive Study of Dispensational Interpretation." (Unpublished doctoral dissertation, Dallas Theological Seminary, 1959).

Lowery, Paul D. "The Character of the Gospel in the Tribulation Period." (Unpublished Master's thesis, Dallas Theological Seminary, 1956).

MacCorkle, Douglas B. "A Study of Amillennial Eschatology." Unpublished Master's thesis, Dallas Theological Seminary, 1947).

MacGown, Philip T. "The Hermeneutics of the Millennial Controversy." (Unpublished Master's thesis, Dallas Theological Seminary, 1952).

Ohman, Raymond N. "The Biblical Doctrine of the Millennium." (Unpublished doctoral dissertation, Dallas Theological Seminary, 1949).

Pentecost, Dwight. "The Judgment of the Nations." (Unpublished Master's thesis, Dallas Theological Seminary, 1941).

Rowe, Harley E. "The Kingdom in Matthew." (Unpublished master's thesis, Dallas Theological Seminary, 1955).

IV. CONTEMPORARY NON-DISPENSATIONALISM

A. BOOKS

Allis, O. T. *Prophecy and the Church.* Philadelphia: The Presbyterian and Reformed Publ. Co., 1945.

Bales, James D. *New Testament Interpretations of Old Testament Prophecies of the Kingdom.* Searcy, Arkansas: The Harding College Press, 1950.

Berkhof, L. *The Second Coming of Christ.* Grand Rapids: Wm. B. Eerdmans Publ. Co., 1953.

Candlish, James S. *The Kingdom of God.* Edinburgh: T. & T Clark, 1884.

Edersheim, Alfred. *Prophecy and History.* Grand Rapids: Baker Publ. Co., 1955.

Fairbairn, Patrick. *Prophecy Viewed in Respect to its Distinctive Nature, Its Special Function, and Proper Interpretation.* Edinburgh: T & T Clark, 1856.

Froom, Le Roy. *The Prophetic Faith of Our Fathers.* 4 vols.; Washington: Review and Herald, 1950.

Fuller, Daniel P. "The Hermeneutics of Dispensationalism." (Unpublished doctoral dissertation, Northern Baptist Theological Seminary, Chicago, Illinois, 1957).

Glasson, T. Francis. *His Appearing and His Kingdom.* London: Epworth Press, 1953.

Hamilton, Floyd. *The Basis of the Millennial Faith.* Grand Rapids: Wm. B. Eerdmans Publ. Co., 1955.

Hatch, H. G. *The Messianic Consciousness of Jesus.* London: SPCK, 1939.

Hodges, Jesse W. *Christ's Kingdom and Coming.* Grand Rapids: Wm. B. Eerdmans, 1957.

Hook, S. H. *The Kingdom of God in the Experience of Jesus.* London: Duckworth, 1949.

Kik, J. Marcellus. *Revelation Twenty.* Philadelphia: Presbyterian & Reformed Publ. Co., 1955.

Bibliography

Matthew Twenty-Four. Philadelphia: Presbyterian & Reformed Publ. Co., 1950.

Klausner, Joseph. *The Messianic Idea in Israel.* New York: Macmillan, 1955.

Kraus, C. Norman. *Dispensationalism in America.* Richmond: John Knox Press, 1958.

Kromminga, D. H. *Millennium in the Church.* Grand Rapids: Wm. B. Eerdmans Publ. Co., 1945.

Kümmel, W. G. *Promise and Fulfillment: The Eschatological Message of Jesus.* Naperville, Ill.: Alec R. Allenson, Inc., 1957.

Ladd, George. *Crucial Question About the Kingdom.* Grand Rapids: Wm. B. Eerdmans Publ. Co., 1952.

————. *The Blessed Hope.* Grand Rapids: Wm. B. Eerdmans Publ. Co., 1956.

————. *The Gospel of the Kingdom.* Grand Rapids: Wm. B. Eerdmans Publ. Co., 1959.

Lenski, R. C. H. *The Interpretation of St. Paul's Exposition of Revelation.* Columbus, Ohio: Lutheran Book Concern, 1936.

Leupold, H. C. *Exposition of Genesis.* Columbus: Wartburg Press, 1942.

Maitland, C. D. *The Apostolic School of Prophetic Interpretation.* London: Longman, Brown, Green and Longman, 1849.

Mauro, Philip. *The Gospel of the Kingdom.* Boston: Hamilton Bros., 1928.

Milton, John P. *Prophecy Interpreted.* Minneapolis: Augsburg Publ. House, 1960.

Pieters, Albertus. *Studies in the Revelation.* Grand Rapids: Wm. B. Eerdmans Publ. Co., 1943.

Ramm, Bernard. *Protestant Bible Interpretation.* Boston: W. A. Wilde & Co., 1950.

Reese, Alexander. *The Approaching Advent of Christ: An Examination of the Teaching of J. N. Darby and His Followers.* London: Marshall, Morgan & Scott, n.d.

Robinson, J. A. T. *Jesus and His Coming: The Emergence of a Doctrine.* New York; Abingdon Press, 1957.

Scott, E. F. *The Kingdom of God in the New Testament.* New York: Macmillan Co., 1931.

Summers, Ray. *Worthy Is The Lamb.* Nashville: Broadman Press, 1951.

Vos, Geerhardus. *The Kingdom and the Church.* Grand Rapids: Wm. B. Eerdmans Publ. Co., 1958 (reprint).

West, Nathaniel. *Premillennial Essays of the Prophetic Conference.* Chicago: Fleming H. Revell Co., 1879.

Wyngaarden, Martin J. *The Future of the Kingdom in Prophecy and Fulfillment.* Grand Rapids: Baker Book House, 1955.

B. PERIODICALS

Allis, O.T. "Modern Dispensationalism and the Doctrine of the Unity of the Scriptures," *Evangelical Quarterly*, 8:22-35, Jan., 1936.

Baillie, John. "Beliefs about the last Things," *Congregational Quarterly*, 28:206-218, July, 1950.

Bear, James E. "Historic Premillennialism," *Union Seminary Review*, Richmond: Union Theological Seminary, 55:193-221, 1944.

——. "Dispensationalism and the Covenant of Grace," *Union Seminary Review*, 44:285-307, July, 1938.

——. "The People of God," *Union Seminary Review*, 52:33-63, Oct. 1940.

——. "The People of God in the Light of the Teaching of the New Testament," *Union Seminary Review*, 55:128-158, Jan., 1941.

——. "The People of God according to the Fathers of the Early Church," *Union Seminary Review*, 52:351-374, Jan., 1941.

Berkouwer, G. C. "The Church in the Last Days," *Christianity Today*, 2:3-5, April 14, 1958.

Bietenhard, H. "Millennial Hope in the Early Church," *Scottish Journal of Theology*, 6:12-30, March, 1953.

Boettner, L. "The Christian Hope and a Millennium," *Christianity Today*, 2:13-14, Sept. 29, 1958.

Bowman, John Wick. "The Bible and Modern Religions: II, Dispensationalism," *Interpretation*, 10:170-187, April, 1956.

Briggs, C. A. "The Origin and History of Premillennialism," *Lutheran Quarterly*, 9:207-245, 1879.

Brown, I. V. "Watchers for the Second Coming: The Millenarian Tradition in America, *"Mississippi Valley Historical Review*, 39:441-458, December, 1958.

Emden, C. S. "Open Secret of the Kingdom of God," *Church Quarterly Review*, 155:281-285, 1954.

Feuillet, A. "Les Vingt-Quarte Vieillards de l'apocalypse," *Revue Biblique*, 65:5-32, Jan., 1958.

Flack, E. E. "Aspects of Christian Eschatology," *Lutheran Quarterly*, 1:369-393, Nov., 1949.

Gilmour, S. M. "The Kingdom and The Church," *Interpretation*, 7:26-33, Jan., 1953.

Grant, R. M. "The Coming of the Kingdom," *Journal of Biblical Literature*, 67:297-303, Dec., 1948.

Grier, W. J. "Christian Hope and the Millennium," *Christianity Today*, 3:18-19, Oct. 13, 1958.

Hodgson, L. "Facts and Interpretation: History and Eschatology," *Church Quarterly Review*, 159:532-547, Oct.-Dec., 1958.

King, W. L. "Millennialism as a Social Ferment," *Religion in Life*, 21:33-44, 1951.

Ladd, G. E. "Eschatology and the Unity of New Testament Theology," *Expository Times*, 68:268-273, June, 1957.

——. "The Revelation of Christ's Glory," *Christianity Today*, 2:13-14, Sept. 1, 1958.

Lawson, M. "Jesus and the Kingdom of God," *Congregational Quarterly*, 3:234-244, July, 1953.

McConnell, Francis J. "The Causes of Premillennialism," *Harvard Theological Review*, 12:179-192, 1919.

McCown. "The Reign of God," *Religion in Life*, 18:211-221, March, 1949.

Mendenhall, G. E. "Covenant forms in Israelite Tradition," *Biblical Archaeologist*, 17:26-46, May, 1954.

Minear, P. S. "Between Two Worlds," *Interpretation*, 5:27-39, Jan., 1951.

Pieters, A. "The Millennial Problem," *The Intelligence-Leader*, 10:432, March, 1943.

Ridderbos, H. N. "Final Triumph: Eternal Kingdom," *Christianity Today*, 2:17-18, June 23, 1958.

Smith, R. H. "Eschatology of Acts and Contemporary Exegesis," *Concordia Theological Monthly*, 29:641-663, Spring, 1958.

Stiegler, M. A. "Dispensations," *Archiv für katholische Kirchenrecht*, 1:3-42, 225-259, 529-551, 649-669. 1897.

INDEX TO SUBJECTS

INDEX TO PERSONS AND PLACES

INDEX TO AUTHORS